DOES THE GOLF DEVIL WHISPER IN YOUR EAR?

Using Your Mind to Play Better and be Happier in Life

Kumiko Rodewald

DOES THE GOLF DEVIL WHISPER IN YOUR EAR?
Using Your Mind to Play Better and be Happier in Life
www.HappyGolferHappyLifeBook.com
Copyright © 2024 Kumiko Rodewald

Paperback ISBN: 979-8-8672-62310

All rights reserved. No portion of this book may be reproduced mechanically, electronically, or by any other means, including photocopying, without permission of the publisher or author except in the case of brief quotations embodied in critical articles and reviews. It is illegal to copy this book, post it to a website, or distribute it by any other means without permission from the publisher or author.

References to internet websites (URLs) were accurate at the time of writing. Authors and the publishers are not responsible for URLs that may have expired or changed since the manuscript was prepared.

Limits of Liability and Disclaimer of Warranty
The author and publisher shall not be liable for your misuse of the enclosed material. This book is strictly for informational and educational purposes only.

Publisher
10-10-10 Publishing
Markham, ON Canada

Printed in Canada and the United States of America

*Dad, I finished the book!
I wish you were still here to read it.
Wait ... you couldn't read it anyway because you didn't speak English! But I know you would've said something funny and been proud of your daughter. Your spirit is always with me when I write.
Love you forever.*

Table of Contents

Testimonials vii
Acknowledgments xiii
Foreword xvii
Introduction xix

Chapter 1: The Secret to Becoming a
Happy Golfer 1
Chapter 2: Magical Transformation 13
Chapter 3: Why Does the Little Golf Ball
Drive You Crazy? 23
Chapter 4: Do You See a Pink Elephant? 31
Chapter 5: Does the Golf Devil Whisper in
Your Ear? 39
Chapter 6: Every Shot Counts 51
Chapter 7: Think Better, Play Better 61
Chapter 8: Do You Hit Crappy Shots? 79
Chapter 9: Unlock the Possibilities 87
Chapter 10: The Secret of Golf 97
Chapter 11: Get into the Zone with a
Zen-Like Mind 105
Chapter 12: Golf Is Like Life 117

About the Author 125

Testimonials

I've been working with Kumiko Rodewald to improve my mental golf game, and the experience has been unbelievable because not only did I shoot five strokes better than my goal just one day after my first session, but my handicap has gone down by about five strokes over the last few months.

Kumiko's coaching style is unique. I wasn't sure if she could help me on Zoom with my golf game, but it really does work! She's helped me gain confidence and improve course management, and my swing and short game are better. I also utilize her mindset technique to slow my swing down.

So, I just want to say that Kumiko is a great coach, and I highly recommend working with her; she can help you improve your golf game the first day you use her techniques.

Kevin Harrington
An original "shark" on the hit TV show
Shark Tank and the American entrepreneur
who invented the infomercial

I struggled a lot with my game before meeting Kumiko. And even though I was practicing twice as much, I couldn't perform to my potential when the tournaments arrived. Then, during one of the first tournaments in my last spring season, I shot one of my highest-ever college scores. I was deeply frustrated with my game and couldn't understand what was happening. I was hitting the ball solidly, and my swing felt harmonious, but my mind wasn't peaceful. There was a lot of pressure because it was my senior year, and I worried too much about not being good enough.

Feeling that the swing and golf talent were there and suspecting I could do much better with guidance, I decided to work more on my mental game immediately following my highest round. My performance improved after only two great sessions with Kumiko, and I lowered my score!

She helped me to control my overthinking on the course and taught me how to control my thoughts from the tee box until the end of the hole. Kumiko didn't just tell me to think "shot by shot," as everyone says. Instead, Kumiko made me analyze my thoughts before every shot and helped me to start thinking about how I was going to make a birdie from every tee box I approached. Not only did I begin to consistently shoot low scores, but I also finished my college career by winning the National Championship. That wouldn't have been possible if I hadn't met Kumiko.

I'm very grateful for all Kumiko has taught me, and I'm excited to continue to improve my game with her help.

Anahi Servin
2022 NCAA Division II
Individual Women's National Champion

If you are looking to get more pars, I highly recommend that you focus between the ears. That's where the game is truly played. To help you with that is Kumiko! She has a true gift for creating relatable tips to help you overcome mental obstacles. She keeps it simple and fun but poignant. She knows her stuff.

Christina Ricci,
PGA\LPGA\TPI 3\Bestselling Golf Author
of *More Pars*

Patience. Ferocity. Resilience. All are needed to be successful on the golf course and in life. Kumiko has done such a wonderful job in her book of teaching us all how we can possess and employ what is necessary to be the best version of ourselves both on and off the golf course.

Known in the industry as a "Golf Therapist" rather than a Mental Coach, Kumiko shares her life experiences and her specific resolve to difficult situations. We get an inside view of how we can positively and powerfully navigate successfully what life and golf present to us so we can be our best! Kumiko is a powerful example for us all to never stop learning or growing!

Brian Jacobs, PGA
Golf Channel Academy, Lead Instructor

The program covered topics so clearly helpful that I was able to deliver demonstrably and solidly better performances for the season. In addition, after completing the program, I could see how "mental" the game truly was and how that affected my performance.

In April 2020, my index was 17.0. By mid-summer, my index was under 9.5! The enjoyment of scoring under 85 and pursuing 80 was just a daydream prior to participating in this program. It is

Testimonials

one of the most rewarding things I've ever done concerning golf game instruction.

Kumiko is a fun, enthusiastic, and knowledgeable coach with a sincere desire to help the golfer who wants that "accountability" needed to achieve their goals.

I have chosen Kumiko to be part of my "team" to help me achieve the goal of shooting par!

Colin Yorke, NY

Kumiko has helped my performance on the golf course by giving me the tools to think and react to situations with clarity and confidence. She has taught me to hit golf shots with a personal approach that gives me the best chance for positive outcomes.

**Chris Johnson,
PGA, Director of Instruction**

I am a senior woman who has enjoyed playing this game for 35 years. Lessons with our club "pros" gave me the swing technique but the "mental side" of the game was always my downfall. However, after participating in Kumiko's mental golf game workshops, I could finally stop beating myself up over a bad round, let a bad swing go (in 10 seconds), move on to the next shot, and really enjoy this game once again. It was as if someone turned the lights on, and I saw that it was me not believing in myself that sent my confidence spiraling downward.

Kumiko has the tools and will help you understand what's needed to play your best once again. She is positive, practical, and doesn't promise you a miracle overnight. I improved with practice and dedication and received our "Most Improved Player" during my classes with Kumiko. It's never too late to improve.

Candice Scharper

Acknowledgments

I first thank my loving parents for all the beautiful memories. And even though Mom and Dad weren't on Earth when I wrote this book, I lit a candle, burned incense, and talked to their photos every morning before working on the manuscript. I believe their spirits were with me and guided me as I wrote.

My sons Jack and Mason supported and encouraged me to make my dream come true. I'm grateful for their caring, loving souls. I couldn't have finished writing without them. I'm the luckiest mom on Earth!

I can't thank enough my writing coach, Clayton Bye. I couldn't have written this book without his support. We met on Zoom every week, and he patiently guided and encouraged me.

Thank you to all my friends who make my life lively with laughter, crying, and sometimes craziness. Distance doesn't matter. Chiaki Mimoto and I live 5,000 miles apart, but we talk every Saturday morning. She often shares her wisdom and sometimes patiently listens to me being a sound bag.

Big hugs to my special Japanese girlfriends, Yumiko Kurokawa, Akiko Kondo, and Kazuko Curtis. We laugh so much together, on and off the course, no matter what's going on in our lives. And, of course, I must thank Mary Hanningsen. She gives me terrific support outside of the golf world. I hope you're "squeezing your boobs" and hitting it great and that you'll start playing with me soon. Love you all.

I must also extend a sincere thank you to my amazing clients, Colin Yorke, Candice Scharper, and Kevin Harrington, who trust and work with me. I learn something valuable during every coaching session with them.

Meghan Tammey, Brian Watts, Dennis McMinn, and Aaron Emch deserve a shout-out for sharing their stories and experiences for my book. Meghan, I'll never forget the story about the guy in red corduroy pants!

Does the Golf Devil Whisper in Your Ear? would never have been written if Jerry Mowlds hadn't taught me how to play golf. Thank you for being patient and telling me to "swing faster" for so many years.

I'm also grateful for the warm support from those wonderful instructors, Brian Jacobs, Christina Ricci, and Chris Johnson. I feel fortunate to have had their mentorship. Thank you!

Acknowledgments

Finally, I want to thank Raymond Aaron. He trusted me, published this book with me, and helped make my dream come true.

Foreword

Kumiko Rodewald is everything you could want to find in an American success story. She came to the United States from Japan to explore American life for one year, not intending to stay and never dreaming of becoming a "Golf Therapist." Yet this remarkable woman took a growing love for the game of golf, became a competitive amateur, and three decades later (still in the US) has developed into an exceptional entrepreneur who teaches serious golfers how to lower their scores—often dramatically—by addressing the mental side of the game.

Kumiko isn't interested in replacing what golf pros and instructors can do for you. Instead, she helps you achieve phenomenal gains by thinking differently about yourself, your golfing ability, the game, and how you manage the course. Kumiko teaches the proven ideas, techniques, and behaviors she used to become a single-digit handicapper so that you can experience similar success.

www.HappyGolferHappyLifeBook.com

I support Kumiko because she's an expert in her marketplace, and I recognize the value she has to offer. If you want to realize more of your potential and play better golf, you need to read this book, follow Kumiko's golfing posts on Facebook, subscribe to her podcast, and hire her as your golf therapist.

Raymond Aaron
***New York Times* Bestselling Author**

Introduction

Does the Golf Devil Whisper in Your Ear? Have you ever been driven crazy as you chased that little white ball over the rolling fairways and treacherous greens? Do you wonder why your short game is so inconsistent, even though you have a solid swing and a great understanding of the game? If you answered yes to any of these questions, chances are the problem isn't your lack of talent or skill. As the great motivator Zig Ziglar used to say, "You've probably got a case of Stinkin' Thinkin'."

Kumiko Rodewald is a mental golf coach who knows from experience that you can transform your golf game by changing what you think and how you think about your game—before you play, while you play, and after you play. She'll teach you that your thoughts aren't always true and can be managed for better play. You can do the same with your beliefs, intent, self-talk, behavior, focus, the way you talk to the ball, and how you manage or navigate the course.

www.HappyGolferHappyLifeBook.com

Chock full of golfing stories and anecdotes, Kumiko's book offers real-life strategies to dramatically improve your golf game. Because contrary to what most people believe, great golf doesn't begin with your swing or stance or how you hold the club. All those things are essential, but the originator of inspired play is your mind. *Does the Golf Devil Whisper in Your Ear?* is your guide to using your mind to play better and be happier in life.

C.C. Bye
Award-winning author and avid golfer

Chapter 1

The Secret to Becoming a Happy Golfer

"Enjoy the game. Happy golf is good golf."
– Gary Player

The Struggling Golfer (Colin's story)

Colin was a typical struggling golfer with a decades-long 17 handicap[1]. A weekend golfer who enjoyed playing with his friends, Colin practiced whenever he could, took the occasional lesson, read articles in the golf magazine, and watched YouTube videos to figure out the latest techniques. He wanted to improve and occasionally shot a better game. But the next time he played,

---

[1] A measure of current ability over an entire round of golf, signified by a number. A handicap essentially signifies how many strokes above or below par a golfer should be able to play. The formula is Handicap = (Handicap Index) (Slope rating/113) + (Course Rating-Par). The lower the number, the better the golfer.

www.HappyGolferHappyLifeBook.com

Colin would fall back to his usual scoring form in the low 90s.

He had more than once declared, "I know I can play at a higher level. I'm athletic and have a decent swing. My game should be better than this."

Words of encouragement or disparagement from fellow golfers meant nothing because the man knew something was missing and had just about given up hope of ever figuring out what that was.

Frustrated and unsure how to improve, he said, "I wish there were magic pills to transform my golf game!"

Colin had heard others say certain things about the mental side of golf, but their words hadn't resonated. So when Colin joined my Facebook group, *Happy Golfer Happy Life*, and saw that I offered members a coaching program for improving their mental golf game, he signed up, attended all four weekly sessions, and applied as much of his learning as possible—the pre-shot routine, picking a specific target, freeing the mind to engage all positive outcomes. He also began keeping a golf journal.

Turns out Colin didn't need the magic pills. Instead, he transformed his golf game using his mind. As a result, the man's handicap plummeted to a single digit in a few months. And now that he's retired and plays more often, his handicap has dropped even further to 6.5.

He said, "Kumiko isn't unlike a therapist. A golf therapist. She creates an intimate relationship where coach and golfer can navigate the obstacles to reach Valhalla in their game."

I'll reveal the secret Colin learned as you read this book.

60,000 Thoughts a Day

According to the research, we have about 60,000 thoughts a day. It sounds like a lot, doesn't it? Studies suggest we can think so many thoughts in a day because 95-98% of our thoughts occur at an unconscious level, and most are repetitive. Sadly, researchers say 80% of them are negative.

No wonder we sometimes feel crappy without knowing why.

Ralph Waldo Emerson once said, "You become what you think about all day long." Many others believe the same thing. To me, this suggests that the next time you feel a little hopeless, you can use your brain to think better and become happier. That's good news!

You're Not Your Thoughts

Wait a minute. Given what I wrote over the last few paragraphs, why would I say you aren't your thoughts? The main reason is that what you think isn't always true. Also, you don't have to believe your thoughts if you don't like them or if they make you feel bad.

For example, what thoughts do you regularly have? To answer this question, please observe and record your thoughts for a while (I suggest a day) without judging, pursuing, or rejecting them. Don't analyze them. Don't argue with them.

When you're finished, I want you to think about each of the thoughts you disliked and ask yourself, "Is this thought true?" Then ask, "Is it helpful?"

How do thoughts affect you, your emotions, and behaviors? If a thought doesn't help or make you feel good, you don't have to believe it. You can ask, "What purpose is the thought serving?" and "How does this thought make me feel?"

One of my clients, Hiro, was an average golfer for 30 years.

He told me, "I only make a couple of birdies a year. That's how it's been for more than ten years."

Then, as part of his work with me to transform his golf game, he started writing his thoughts and beliefs about his game on paper. He kept it up and recorded as many thoughts as he could. One of them was about making birdies. Hiro believed making a birdie happens only a few times a year.

I asked, "Is that true?"

His answer was, "It seems like being true to me."

I said, "You don't have to hit perfect shots or play like a tour pro on TV to make a birdie. You just have to hit straight with the right distance and make a putt, especially on a par 3. You can also make a lucky birdie."

That helped Hiro change his negative belief to a positive one, which made him feel more optimistic and excited. Within a couple of weeks, he made a birdie. Then he made another. Now, making birdies is no longer a special event, and he goes for them whenever he has an opportunity.

What thoughts are keeping you from transforming your golf game?

www.HappyGolferHappyLifeBook.com

No Pill Can Fix Your Golf Game. Use Your Mind Instead

Do you often wish you could pop a pill in your mouth, magically disappear your problems, and play extraordinary golf? Unfortunately, it's not going to happen. But while there are no magic pills to fix your golf game, you already have magical power within you. It's your mind! Your mind can do much for your golf game, including improving your swing and short game, course management, handling your emotions, setting goals, forming clear intentions, and getting in the zone. As a result, you'll enjoy more golf and become a happier golfer.

However, golfers often focus on mechanics and aren't aware of the rest of the game.

Hiro was a typical golfer who focused on how to swing, chip, and putt. When he hit a bad shot and missed a putt, he usually blamed it on his mechanics. Hiro never connected that he hit a bad shot because he didn't aim at the target. Instead, he blamed out-of-bounds (OB) lies on the swing (OB is marked with white stakes, and play is prohibited in that area). He also thought and worried about OB shots on many fairways, which put his focus on "OB" rather than where he wanted to hit. Now that he knows the secret, he hardly worries about OB shots.

You'll learn what Hiro learned as you keep reading this book, and you'll transform your golf game, too.

Smile and Become a Happy Golfer

Sarah was a happy golfer, although she wasn't the best golfer in their circle. A positive thinker, she always had a smile, no matter how horrible she played. Sarah's smile not only made her feel better but lifted everyone in their group. Her friends often wondered what Sarah's secret to happiness was.

Would you be surprised to learn that Sarah's secret was something incredibly simple? **She was grateful to be with her friends on a beautiful golf course!** It sounds too good to be true, but smiling makes you happy! Even a fake smile can trick your brain into thinking you're happy.

According to Dr. Isha Gupta, a neurologist from IGEA Brain and Spine, a smile produces a chemical reaction in the brain and releases certain hormones, including dopamine and serotonin. Dopamine is known as the "happy hormone." Serotonin helps you to reduce stress. Smiling can also lower your heart rate and blood pressure in tense situations. There's also evidence that it leads to a longer life! It has even been scientifically proven that smiling is contagious! It has the power to change your mood and the moods of others.

No one knows whether Sarah was aware of this science and used smiling to make herself and others happy or if that was her nature. Either way, she made everyone's round better. And what could be more noble in this life than to leave people better than you found them?

When you aren't playing well, and happiness has disappeared along with your ball, smile! Even if you don't feel like it, smile. Fake it 'til you feel it and spread the happy vibe to others.

You Become What You Believe

"You become what you believe, not what you think or what you want," is a beautiful Oprah Winfrey quote.

What do you believe about your golf game and life? Have you ever wanted to give up on golf? I think most golfers have had a moment like that at least once.

Golf is like life. Sometimes it isn't easy, and it's often painful and cruel. You can lose hope and start doubting yourself and your ability. You might even feel defeated or like a failure. So, I ask, "What dreams and goals do you have that you don't feel you can achieve?"

The Secret to Becoming a Happy Golfer

Daniel dreamed of being a single-digit handicapper, but his average scores were in the 90s with an occasional high 80s. It was hard for him to believe his dream could come true. He thought a low handicap was for talented people. And the closer he got to his 60th birthday, the harder it became to keep his dream alive.

After Daniel learned the secret, he wrote down all the limiting beliefs that were getting in the way of achieving his goals. One of them was that he couldn't become a single-digit handicapper.

He had been asking himself, *How can I possibly become a single-digit handicapper? I've been shooting 90s!*

Now he wondered, *How do I know I can't do this?*

It was a question Daniel couldn't answer, so he decided to apply the methods he learned from my program and started taking small steps.

He nurtured positive thoughts like, *I bet I can be a single-digit handicapper if I keep working on it.*

And the better he played, the more Daniel believed he could achieve his goal.

You're just getting old!

Mike was a low handicapper in his mid-50s, and though he was better than most players on the planet, he wanted to improve his game and shoot lower scores. Instead, his game worsened, and he began to doubt his ability.

His golf buddies said, "You're just getting old. Everyone hits shorter and plays worse as they age."

Mike didn't want to believe them, but their words had weight.

He thought, *I guess they're right. I'm hitting shorter, and it has been hard to shoot lower scores.*

Then Mike learned about reframing limiting beliefs and decided to try it.

The first belief that came to mind was, *I hit shorter and play worse as I get older.*

Mike felt sick to his stomach.

He sat still, closed his eyes, took a deep breath, and asked himself, *Why do I believe that?*

Here's what Mike wrote down:

- *Most golfers, including my golf buddies, think the reality is you play worse as you age.*
- *Is it true?*
- *That's what they believe, but I'm not sure it's true. Some people keep playing well, and some even get better as they age. I just need to focus on myself and my game and keep working on it. I don't have to believe what they believe.*

Next, Mike came up with three statements that could support his goal to improve his golf game and

The Secret to Becoming a Happy Golfer

shoot lower scores:

1. *I keep improving my game.*
2. *Age doesn't affect my game!*
3. *I'm becoming the best golfer I've ever been.*

Mike read the three affirmations every day. He felt better and started believing he could improve. It wasn't long before that became his reality!

Here's an exercise for you:

- Grab a piece of paper or notebook and sit quietly for a while.
- See how many beliefs you can write down that block you from making your dreams come true or achieving your goals.
- For each belief, ask yourself, "What makes me believe this?" Then ask, "Is it true?" If your answer is yes, ask, "How do I know it's true?" You don't have to keep beliefs if you don't like them.
- Dig deeper until you reframe the limiting beliefs in a way that allows you to begin believing in your new thoughts a little more than before.
- Write down your new beliefs and read and say them as affirmations.
- Repeat this exercise as often as you wish.

In the next chapter, I'll share how I managed to transform from an average female recreational golfer shooting between 90 and 100 to a 7 handicapper in one year.

Chapter 2

Magical Transformation

"Miracles happen to those who believe in them."
– Bernard Berenson

Swing Backwards

I'm not a talented golfer and actually hated golf when I was a kid. But I was an active girl and loved to play with boys outside. So when I was about ten, my dad came home with a little set of kids' golf clubs.

He said, "You're going to play golf now."

My dad wasn't a great golfer, but he loved the game. I remember he didn't mind getting up early to play nine holes before work.

I looked at one of the clubs and wondered if he got the wrong set because they were right-handed clubs (I'm pure left-handed like my dad).

"Dad, you got the wrong clubs!"

"Sorry, girl. They don't make left-handed clubs for kids."

I thought that wasn't fair! My dad had perfect clubs that swung in the right direction, so why did I have to swing backwards? It didn't make sense, and I hated the idea. It was the beginning of the disaster that was my childhood golf.

A Golfer with a Fancy Golf Bag and No Clubs

I played tennis in middle school and made the high school team. I practiced hard and loved it. Unfortunately, Dad wouldn't let me give up golf (given the perspective of time, I think his dream was to play golf with his daughter).

My memories aren't clear, but I know I resented Dad for making me practice my swing in the yard and play golf with him and, sometimes, his friends. I thought it boring to play with old men. They might've been in their early 40s, but they were old in my mind.

I wasn't a typical rebellious teen, yet I became one where golf was concerned. All I cared about was looking good in cute golf clothes and playing with colorful, candy-like golf balls with matching tees. Despite my attitude, my dad made me keep up with the pace of play, and I know I looked pretty unhappy on the course.

Magical Transformation

That went on for years. Dad refused to give up on playing golf with me, and I didn't cave. My 20th birthday came and went, and I still didn't own a set of golf clubs. All I had was a fancy golf bag. So when I played with my dad, I grabbed Mom's beautiful, red-shafted clubs and slipped them into that fancy bag.

I had colorful balls, cute clothes, and nice golf shoes, but I was careless about my game.

Go From Shooting 100 to a 7 Handicap in One Year!

I played more golf after I moved to the US in my early 20s, mainly for social reasons. There was still no passion for the game. Nevertheless, I shot consistently in the low hundreds, occasionally broke 100, and now owned a set of clubs.

Life was a struggle. I lived in a foreign country and spoke limited English. I was scared to pick up the phone, terrified to buy meat by the pound at the counter in the grocery store. People thought I was quiet, but I didn't say much because I didn't understand what they were saying! It was frustrating, and I felt like I had lost my identity and purpose in life. Then I developed a medical condition that required two surgeries in six months. At the end of it all, doctors told me it would be virtually impossible to get pregnant. I was devastated.

I had grown up as a goal-oriented person but now had nothing to work toward. So I began to seek something tangible into which I could put my energy and effort, something where I could see actual results. I'm not sure what the trigger was, but one day, I decided to set the goal of becoming a single-digit handicapper in one year. I thought it was reasonable because I 100% believed anyone could achieve the same goal—if they took lessons, practiced, and played often. I didn't doubt it at all.

As luck would have it, I landed a great teacher, Jerry Mowlds, and could practice and play a lot. My game quickly improved, and I was soon shooting 80 consistently. Now the challenge was to break 80, but the more I tried, the more difficult that hurdle seemed. I started playing better on the back nine (37) but continued shooting 45 on the front nine. It took me more than a few rounds to break 80, and then I returned to shooting 80. It was as if I had that program in my system.

I still remember my joy when I shot a 79 for the first time! However, shortly after hitting that milestone, I played my first outside competition. I was nervous, and it was a disaster. I shot 88 for both rounds, coming last in the field. I could barely keep a smile on my face until I got in my car. On my way home, I admit that I cried. It hurt so much, especially when I remembered my teacher saying, "Kumiko, the good players shoot lower scores even on bad days."

Magical Transformation

My journey continued, though, and I refused to doubt that I could achieve my goal of getting down to a single-digit handicap. Within a year, my handicap was down to 7!

Later, when I understood more about golf, it became apparent that my belief that "anyone can be a single-digit handicapper if they take lessons, practice, and play often" was uncommon. My ignorance had led me to the lucky conviction that such a thing was, without a doubt, possible. It taught me an invaluable lesson.

If you believe in yourself, have a crystal-clear intention, and take action, anything is possible. The mind is that powerful!

A Prisoner of War (POW) Story

His name is Major James Nesmeth, an average golfer who shot in the mid to low nineties—the typical weekend golfer who wasn't exceptional but loved the game.

Nesmeth was a combat pilot who flew missions over North Vietnam during the Vietnam War. Unfortunately, he was captured and became a POW. He spent the next seven years imprisoned in a small cage where he didn't have much space to move around. He didn't see anyone, didn't talk to anyone, and was allowed no physical activity.

For the first few months, all Nesmeth did was hope and pray for release or rescue. Then he began playing on his favorite golf course every day—in his mind. He didn't play for fun; he did it to keep sane. He visualized as many details as possible: what he was wearing, the smell of fresh-cut grass, and how the sun and breezes felt on his skin. Saw the trees, heard the birds, picked up his club, did a pre-shot routine, took a practice swing, addressed the ball, imagined the perfect shot landing in the center of the fairway in his mind, and hit the ball.

Before his captivity, James Nesmeth played golf to escape from a hectic, everyday life. And he enjoyed every moment of the game. Is it any wonder he did the same thing in his mind when forcibly restrained in a cage? James felt every step and even stopped to sip the water as if he was playing an actual round. He went deep and played exceptional golf in his mind every day for seven years. It made him feel good—at least when he drifted away from his grim reality to golf in his imagination.

After seven long years of captivity, James was finally released and returned to the US. His health had deteriorated because of the poor living conditions he endured for so many years, but soon after returning home, he decided to play golf at his favorite course. James shot a two-over, 74! That meant he shaved 20 strokes off his average after not having swung the club for seven years!

Certainly, this last story is an extreme and unusual example of the power of the mind. But you can't deny that it demonstrates you can improve your golf game with your mind and without physical activity. So, when you can't play golf (even if you're a daily player), spend some time visualizing a perfect round at your favorite course. Experience the game in your mind as if you're actually playing. Be specific and use as many details as you can. You and your buddies might be in for a surprise!

You're Far More Capable Than You Think

I don't think Major James Nesmeth expected to play incredible golf—even though he had imagined thousands of rounds. James was an average golfer before seven years of captivity and limited physical activity, so shooting a 74—a score most of us only dream about—had to have been quite a shock. Nesmith had stumbled upon a secret that helps today's elite athletes improve their performance through "mental rehearsal."

Your mind can't tell the difference between actual experience and the imagined!

We see Olympic athletes put on headphones and close their eyes before performing. They're busy creating a mental picture of what they're about to see, feel, hear, and smell. They're practicing and executing their best performance in their mind. Because these athletes have learned that we remember what's clearly imagined just as well as what we do.

And guess what? Both positive and negative mental rehearsal affect your performance. If you think, *I don't want to 3 putt,* or *I chunk with an iron all the time,* or *I slice off with a driver,* you'll most likely picture the situation and feel it. The more often and the more clearly you think negatively, the more likely that's what you'll do. Such thoughts color what you feel, what you do, and what you experience. So, not only can you create a good habit through positive thinking and visualization, but it's also possible to create a poor habit. It's the truth behind an idea expressed by a saying you may have heard: "Whatever the mind can conceive and believe, it can achieve." Bottom line? You're more capable than you think.

Here's an exercise I would like you to do:

- Write down five things you want to perform at your very best. Make sure the statement is positive. For example, say, "I want to hit a straight

solid shot," rather than, "I don't want to hit OB." Be specific.
- Visualize each performance in as much detail as possible, including the emotions you want to put into play. You want the experience to be as real as possible.
- How do you feel?

Have fun with this exercise. The key is "feeling." You want to feel good—just as Major James Nesmeth did in prison. Your mind is so much more powerful than you know!

Believe in the Power Within You, and Magical Things Can Happen

What do you believe about yourself? Do you believe you're capable of being the golfer you want to be? What is the ideal you as a golfer? I ask these questions because we often limit ourselves even before we try. We give up because we don't believe we can make it happen. Even worse, we sometimes believe what other people tell us: "You're too old to hit longer. We all lose distance as we get older," or "You need to practice hitting a lot of balls to get better," or "You need to start young if you want to be a good golfer." The list can go long!

Everything starts in your mind.

As Henry Ford said, "If you think you can do a thing or think you can't do a thing, you're right." Whether you believe you can make magical things happen or you're a failure, you have the power to make your beliefs come true.

And Bruce Lee said, "As you think, so shall become." You must believe you can achieve if you're to get what you want.

> **If there are no limitations, what kind of golfer and person do you want to be?**
> **Don't limit yourself in your mind, and magical things can happen!**

Chapter 3

Why Does the Little Golf Ball Drive You Crazy?

*"Golf is a game whose aim is to hit a very small ball into an even smaller hole,
with weapons singularly ill-designed for the purpose."*
– Winston Churchill

Have you ever noticed that your little golf ball seems to be acting as if it has a mind of its own? Sometimes it smiles at you and gives you such joy and makes you so happy. On other days it's out of control and acts as if possessed by an evil spirit. You start breathing shallow and feel like you might pass out, or you become so angry that you fear you're about to lose your mind. Then there are the days when the ball teases you, going up and down and putting you on an emotional roller coaster ride.

Steve's Roller Coaster Story

Steve is a happy guy with enthusiastic energy. He enjoys the game of golf and especially loves to play with his buddies. When Steve makes a tee time, he always gets as excited as a little boy before going on a field trip.

On this particular day, he goes to the driving range and hits well. A big smile forms on his face.

I'm ready for tomorrow. I can feel that I'm going to play great.

The following day, Steve wakes up before the alarm goes off.

What a beautiful morning! It's going to be a great golf day!

His mind is already at the golf course, and when he actually arrives, he decides to warm up on the driving range. He begins with the wedge.

Not bad.

Still hitting well, his expectations of a great game rise even higher. Steve now walks over to the practice green. The green looks nice and smooth, and the ball rolls nicely.

Hmm, it's a little faster than the greens I usually play.

Steve's buddies arrive, and they excitedly head to the first tee. Steve grabs his driver from his bag with much anticipation.

He says, "This is going to be great!"

Why Does the Little Golf Ball Drive You Crazy?

The man takes a couple of practice swings and does his best to move the way he did on the range earlier. He makes solid contact with pure sound, but his ball decides to go to the right side of the hole and rolls past the white OB stakes.

"NOoo!" he screams. "Why? I didn't hit like this on the range!"

Gone is his earlier excitement.

The second hole is a short par 3. Still upset from the OB on the first tee, Steve hits the shot without much effort. He doesn't make solid contact, but it soars straight and stops 10 feet from the pin.

Okay! A 2 putt for par would be great.

He doesn't read the green much, but this time, Steve's ball decides to disappear into the cup.

Wow!!! Yay. Birdie! Maybe I can turn this around.

And Steve starts thinking. Becomes more cautious. He nervously tees up on the third hole. There are trees close on the right side.

"Don't hit to the right," he says over and over again as if it's a mantra.

The man timidly attempts to guide the ball so he doesn't hit to the right, but the ball rushes deep into the woods.

Steve cries out, "No! Why?" and his friends do their best not to laugh at his animated reaction.

In all fairness, Steve isn't the kind of guy who gets angry. But he's terribly frustrated. Finally arriving on the green, he's left with a 4-footer for a double bogey.

At least I make this and walk off with a double.

He starts discussing the line with his buddies, although they're not supposed to read the line for each other. It's a friendly game, so they ignore the rule.

"It's pretty straight," one of them says.

"I see it breaks to the right," says another.

"It's faster than you think," offers up the third friend.

Now Steve is confused, and he putts with uncertainty. The ball is uncooperative and decides to stop a couple of inches from the cup. The emotional roller coaster ride continues.

Does Steve's story sound familiar? I bet we've all been there and can relate.

On the other hand, have you ever thought about what's really going on? Is it the ball or luck or you? I believe the results we get in golf and life involve deciding for yourself what your experience means. After all, does a terrible shot mean you're destined to do it again?

The Luckiest Bounce

There's nothing you can do with good luck or bad luck. It just is.

LPGA player Mika Miyazato got one of the luckiest bounces I've ever witnessed. It was a beautiful northwest summer day in August 2012. Mika was playing in the final round at the LPGA Safeway classic. She was a great player who always wore a cute smile, and I felt a positive vibe from her. The 11th hole was a par 3 with a little creek along the fairway and the green. Mika pushed her tee shot toward the water, but the ball miraculously hit a rock in the creek, bounced high, and stopped on the green. She ended up winning by two shots for the tournament! Who knows what would've happened without the lucky bounce? If she had been unlucky, her ball would have stayed in the creek, her drop would have resulted in a bad lie, and she would have made a double bogey.

It's a mistake to expect good or bad luck. Lady Luck visits and leaves us regardless of the level we play. Golf is like life. The best thing you can do is to accept whatever happens, let it go, and move on to the next shot. And when you get lucky, be thankful for the Golf God and enjoy the moment!

Thousands of Golf Balls
Went Swimming in the Pond

On one of those perfect, beautiful, late fall afternoons, I decided to play 9 holes by myself. It was a quiet walk with no one around until I saw the young guy in the pond on par 3.

"Why are you swimming in the beautiful water?" I asked sarcastically as he treaded in the dirty, muddy pond. I had no desire to join him.

"I'm a diver. I'm getting the balls in the water. It's a little cold today."

He must have collected thousands of golf balls. Most were white, but I saw some pink, orange, and yellow ones.

"I'm pretty sure more than a few of my smiley face balls are in there," I said.

I bet most of the balls were hit into the water by sad, unhappy golfers like myself, and I wondered if there were stories to each ball. I would love to ask them questions.

They would say things like:

- "I love swimming. I'd rather be in the water than getting walloped so many times!"
- "Thank God! I finally got away from the abuser. He was so mean to me."
- "I'm sad to say goodbye to her. She was very nice."

Have you ever thought of what your golf ball would say about you? What would it say to other little golf balls in the water?

Why Does the Little Golf Ball Drive You Crazy?

That Little Golf Ball has a Mind of its Own

That little ball you chase around the golf course seems to have a mind. On a good day, the ball listens to you and behaves just as you want. But watch out if it's in a bad mood! The experience can be so powerful that some of us talk to the ball as if it listens and has a soul and spirit.

The weird thing is that sometimes the ball does listen to you. It finds the hole from 30 feet for a birdie or 150 yards for a hole-in-one. Then you forget everything good or bad that happened on previous holes or even what's going on in your life. Instead, you're filled with joy and exist only in the moment. It's experiences like this that keep you playing golf. We all seek happiness—on the golf course and in life.

Everyone hits good and bad shots, whether playing on the tour, as a weekend golfer, or just new to the game. You can't control those results. What you <u>can</u> do is control your behavior before the shot. You can do your best, accept the outcome, let go of whatever you did, and move on to the next shot. Golf legend Ben Hogan once said, "The most important shot in golf is the next one."

Do You Talk to Your Golf Ball?

As previously mentioned, some of us talk to the ball. We command. We plead. We beg. We yell. It's as if you're talking to the dog...

"Sit."

"Get over."

"Stay out."

"Don't go."

"Go straight."

You may even utter commands like, "Get in there!" to someone else's golf ball. How goofy-weird that must seem to non-golfers.

Maybe. But there's no denying that your emotions go up or down with the little ball's behavior.

According to quantum physics, **everything is energy.** Albert Einstein once said, "Everything is energy, and that's all there is to it. Match the frequency of the reality you want, and you cannot help but get that reality. It can be no other way."

So, if you're a person who talks to the ball, be nice to it and treat it as your best friend. I put a smiley face on my golf ball. It always smiles at me, even when I hit a bad shot or run into bad luck. I've been playing with smiley golf balls for decades. Who knows, your golf ball might have a certain energy with magical powers—if you believe in it.

Chapter 4

Do You See a Pink Elephant?

"Once the subconscious mind accepts an idea, it begins to execute it."
– Joseph Murphy

I want you to close your eyes and picture a pink elephant. Do you see a pink elephant? Do you see clearly? What shade of pink is it? Hot pink, regular pink, or pastel color? Is the elephant a real one or a cartoon-like Dumbo with big ears? How about the size? I bet you can create more than one image of pink elephants.

We'll come back to this exercise in a little while.

Lisa's Story (Don't Slice the Ball)

Lisa enjoys playing with her friends in the weekly ladies group. She plays for fun and has been playing for a long time. Lisa does wish she could play better but has no clue how to do that. She has taken an occasional lesson and goes to the range to work on what she learned from the instructor, but it hasn't improved her game.

Lisa's main problem is her habit of coming over the top, which creates a slice.

She's tried to overcome the tendency and often says, "Lisa, don't slice. Don't come over the top." Sadly, Lisa hasn't stopped slicing.

Out on the practice range, she whispers, "Please don't slice." But before she knows it, the bucket's empty, and she sighs disappointedly.

Why can't I get better?

As usual, Lisa plays with her friends on Tuesday. She enjoys herself, but the harder she tries to eliminate the slice, the more she finds the right side of the course. She's hopeless.

Why can't I stop slicing? I took a lesson and practiced hard!

Lisa decides to take another lesson and find another way not to slice the ball. She sends a text message to her instructor to book a lesson.

The Unconscious (Subconscious) Mind Controls More Than 95% of Your Life

As mentioned in the first chapter, 95-98% of our 60,000 daily thoughts occur subconsciously, 80% of which are primarily repetitive negative thoughts. It's hard to comprehend, isn't it?

Furthermore, have you thought about how our mind works? The conscious mind is your objective or thinking mind. It has no memory and can only hold one thought at a time. The subconscious mind is a different creature. It's a container of the thoughts, feelings, urges, and memories that exist beneath our conscious awareness. The neurologist Freud used the iceberg as a metaphor to explain the concept. He referred to the conscious mind as the "tip of the iceberg" that shows above the water. The rest of the iceberg hidden beneath the water represents the subconscious mind. It's a surprisingly accurate comparison.

Here are more interesting facts about our subconscious mind:

- It can't tell the difference between imagination and reality.
- The subconscious mind can't process the word "don't." For example, if you say, "Don't slice the ball," it processes, "Slice the ball."
- It responds a few hundred milliseconds before the conscious mind.
- Emotions are messages from the subconscious mind.

Now, let's dive in deeper and learn how to use your mind to play better and feel better...

Did You Eat the Leftover Chicken in the Fridge?

Sam was hungry but had nothing to eat at home, and he was feeling too lazy to eat out or go to the grocery store. He rechecked the fridge just in case he had overlooked something to eat. He found some fried chicken that belonged to his roommate, Matt.

It doesn't look that great, but it will do.

Sam put the chicken in the microwave without thinking about how Matt would react. When it was hot, he took the chicken out of the microwave and began eating mindlessly.

Then Matt walked into the room and screamed, "Don't eat it! It's old. You'll get sick, dude!"

Immediately, Sam felt nauseated.

"Oh, my God! It doesn't taste right. Why did you keep the old chicken in the fridge?"

Matt laughed and said, "I got you! It's not old. But don't eat my food! The next time, you might get sick for real."

You see, as soon as Matt told Sam the chicken was old and would make him sick, Sam created that story in his mind. The subconscious mind acted on the imagined scene, and his body responded with the built-in response for ejecting "Old food that will make me sick."

We do similar things all day long when thinking about something that has already happened or imagining something that might occur in the future. It's as true on the golf course as in daily life.

I want you to think of one of the best moments of your golf game. Perhaps you made a hole-in-one, hit your best drive ever, shot your lowest score, or sank a 50-foot putt. How do you feel when you think about it? I bet you feel great! That's your imagination, and even though it happened in the past, your mind makes you feel good. The same thing can happen when you recall painful events. So, be aware of what you think. Whether your thoughts are about actual or imagined experiences, make them positive, and you'll feel better!

Don't Picture a Pink Elephant

Let's go back to the pink elephant idea, but this time I want you to close your eyes and try your best not to picture that pink elephant. DO NOT picture a pink elephant!

I'm willing to bet that most of you saw a pink elephant in your mind. You probably saw the pink elephant you imagined earlier and changed to a different color of elephant or switched to a giraffe. Because the unconscious mind doesn't recognize the word "don't." That's why when you tell yourself, *"Don't hit OB,"* or *"Don't 3 putt,"* or *"Don't slice into the water,"* you tend to do exactly what you didn't want to do.

Lisa kept telling herself, *"Don't come over the top. Don't slice."*

Her subconscious only heard, *"Come over the top. Slice."*

The next time you practice or play, observe what you tell yourself and what others say out loud to themselves. We all tend to tell ourselves what not to do mindlessly. And you would be surprised how often you say those negative statements out loud. I suggest that you begin saying positive statements during the round. You might shave a few strokes off your scorecard!

Beach Day on the Course

Jim isn't the best sand player. Whenever he gets into the bunker, his heart starts racing, and he feels his body temperature rising. The man works hard to avoid the bunkers, but there's more than one sand trap on every hole at the course he plays.

Do You See a Pink Elephant?

Today, on the first hole, Jim tried hard not to hit the green side bunker. He told himself, *I'm not going to hit into the bunker all day today.* But that tiny white ball got sucked into the sand despite his wish, and his spirit slipped downward as he walked down the fairway.

The man rallied when he addressed the ball, saying, "You got this, Jim!" However, once again, that little white ball had a different idea and decided to stay in the bunker so Jim could enjoy the sand shot a few more times.

The second was a short par 3 with a big green with a couple of tiny bunkers. Jim knew the hole presented no real danger and said, "I got this hole. The bunkers are tiny, and the green is huge!" Still, he couldn't stop thinking about the bunkers with fear.

Jim hit a decent shot. Except his ball didn't want to get on the green; it seemed to enjoy the beach. "Why?" he yelled, "The bunker is tiny!"

One of his buddies grinned and said, "Hey, you're having a beach day. Do you need a drink?"

He groaned, and as his friend suspected, Jim raked the bunkers all day.

Does Jim's story sound familiar to you?

I played with a few of my girlfriends today, and one of them kept saying, "I'm having a beach day!" Her ball was sucked into the bunkers as if they had some special magnetic force.

So many of us are terrified of sand shots, which is interesting since many greenside bunkers are smaller than greens. Logically, it should be easier to hit the larger green than the bunker. So what's going on?

In Jim's case, fear of bunkers created a mental image of hitting the ball and landing in the bunker. Then he kept thinking, *Don't hit into the bunker,* which the subconscious mind processed as the command, *Hit into the bunker.* Jim certainly tried hard to hit the green with his conscious mind, but the subconscious responded first.

We often experience the same issue on the golf course and in life, and changing may seem hopeless. But there's good news. You can use the process in a positive way to get good results and feel great! You'll become a better golfer and be happier. More on this in the upcoming chapters.

You'll improve your game and life if you learn how the conscious and subconscious minds work and apply some proven tricks and tools!

Chapter 5

Does the Golf Devil Whisper in Your Ear?

"They call it golf because all the other four-letter words were taken."
– Ray Floyd

The Golf Devil on Mike's Shoulder

Mike wakes up in anticipation and excitement. Today is the first round of the club championship at the club he belongs to. Mike has worked hard on his game the past few months and has gotten so much better that he gained confidence and started trusting his swing. He has come very close to winning the title in the past and tells himself, *"I'm going to be a champion this year!"*

Mike feels pretty good walking to the first tee despite the little butterfly in his stomach.

The golf angel whispers, "Everyone gets a butterfly

in their stomach in competition—even the pros on TV. You got this, Mike."

He feels a little shaky, but he manages to land his tee shot in the middle of the fairway.

"Good job, Mike," says the golf angel.

He pulls with his second shot, and his ball flies into the green side bunker. Now, the golf devil appears on Mike's shoulder.

"You're an idiot! What are you doing?"

Mike's not the best bunker player, but the golf angel still attempts to comfort him, saying, "You can do it! You just need to get out and put the ball on the green."

Except he's nervous and afraid of chunking it. The image of chunking the ball forms in his mind, and he does exactly what he pictured.

The golf devil raises its voice and says, "Oh, my god! You're horrible. You never hit a good shot from the bunker."

The man started with a double, but now the golf angel has disappeared. To make matters worse, the golf devil decides to stay on his shoulder for the rest of the day.

"Why did you miss the putt, Mike? You choked again. I knew you would miss it. You always miss 4-footers. You can't putt."

"There's the hazard on the left; don't hook it like you always do."

"What's wrong with you?"

Does the Golf Devil Whisper in Your Ear?

"I know you're going to chunk it."

"Don't you dare to think you're better than you are! There are so many good players in this tournament. No way you can win."

And as the golf devil keeps whispering in his ear, Mike's confidence diminishes. He nears the end of the round, beat up and feeling defeated. He's disappointed, frustrated, and hopeless.

He thinks, *Why can't I play better? I worked so hard on my game for this tournament. I hate golf!*

The golf devil grins and replies, "You're such a wimp. You should quit!"

On and on it goes, whispering abuse, putting Mike down, and offering suggestions that generate fear, doubt, and frustration until the golfer feels hopeless.

It whispers, "I'm staying on your shoulder tomorrow, too."

⋯⋙⋅⋘⋯

I bet every golfer has had the golf devil sit on a shoulder and whisper in their ear all day. How often have you heard the exclamation, "You're such an idiot!" or something more colorful? I bet you've even heard the "F-bomb" dropped so emphatically that it traveled to the next hole. The golf devil sometimes yells and screams and drives you to throw your club (I've witnessed someone throw his club so hard that the iron got stuck in the tree).

The golf devil can destroy your confidence, trust, and golf game, and alter your behavior. Its whispers get into your head, and you unconsciously create images and develop feelings based on what it says. Think of it as a "negative mental rehearsal" where you tell yourself to do the things you want to avoid. It's so upsetting and frustrating that the devil on your shoulder often keeps whispering until the golf angel shows up to rescue you.

You Aren't What the Golf Devil Says to You

Do you believe everything the golf devil (negative self-talk) says to you? Is what it tells you true?

The golf devil told Mike, "You always miss 4-footers. You can't putt." And I'm confident you'll have had a similar experience. So, think about it…

Is it true that you ALWAYS miss 4-footers? Always? Of course not. You've made a 4-foot putt many times, and you've made longer putts, too. Everyone misses short putts, but not every time. So the dialogue isn't true.

You can say to yourself (and the little devil on your shoulder), *"Missing this putt doesn't mean I always miss a 4-footer. I've made lots of putts like this. Even the pros on TV sometimes miss a short putt. So, I'll just let it go and do my best next time. Yes … I … can … putt!"*

That's how you call the golf angel to sit on your shoulder, smile, and give you the power of self-love and positivity.

Now consider the golf devil's statement, "There are so many good players in this tournament. No way you can win."

If Mike asked himself if it was true, he would probably have answered, *"Yes, it's true there are many good players in this tournament, and I've never won."* That's not the best approach. Should you ever find yourself in such a situation, you might want to take a couple of deep breaths and ask, *"Does it have to be true? Do I want it to be true?"*

The important thing is to jolt yourself into changing the dialogue. For example, you could think, *I've never won, and there are a lot of good players, but it's not true that I can't win. You just never know. I've been working on my game, and I'm capable of winning. I just need to do my best and focus on my game.*

"You got this," the golf angel whispers.

Say Thank You and Goodbye to the Golf Devil

It may seem counterintuitive, but the golf devil's intention is to help you. It thinks it's doing a great job and doesn't want you hurt. The problem is that its primary tools are fear and anxiety. You don't need that kind of help. Negative talk doesn't help you play better or feel better. Remember our discussion about how the subconscious mind works? You want to use your mind to create positive outcomes and feelings.

So, what do you do? Instead of chasing away the little devil with a golf club, I suggest you take a moment to form the thought, *I know you're trying to help me, but I don't need your support anymore. Thank you for taking care of me.*

You see, resisting or pushing away negative thoughts and feelings isn't a good idea. The psychiatrist Carl Jung once said, "What you resist persists." Let the golf devil whisper without pushing it away and then think, *Thank you and goodbye.*

It may seem silly to talk with an imaginary devil, but the metaphor works. It's much easier to picture a tiny devil whispering in your ear than to visualize the concept of negative self-talk.

Hello, Golf Angel

When the golf devil leaves, the golf angel sometimes shows up with loving and positive energy. Consider Jennifer, who started playing golf because she and her husband, Paul, are empty nesters. Paul is an avid golfer, so when their youngest daughter left for college, Jennifer thought golf would be something they could enjoy together.

Paul signed Jennifer up for the women's golf workshop, but she wasn't sure she was good enough to attend the event. However, her uncertainty manifested positively as the thought, *Paul supports the idea of me wanting to play golf. Maybe I should go.*

There were 15 women at the event—most new to golf, like Jennifer. The instructors were friendly and patient, and she was hitting much better by the end of the lesson.

How exciting!

Next, there was a mental golf workshop. That surprised Jennifer. She thought the mental game was for high-performance players, not beginners like her. Nevertheless, she had a blast in the workshop, learning tips she could apply next time she played.

Now, I can enjoy playing golf with Paul no matter what happens in the game. I know <u>how</u> to play!

One beautiful fall day, Jennifer headed to the golf course with her husband. The beauty of the vivid red, yellow, and orange colored leaves on the trees surrounding the course was stunning.

Paul said, "Wow. So pretty. It's going to be a wonderful day."

Despite the wonder around them, Jennifer began to feel nervous as they began walking to the first tee.

She whispered, "You got this. My goal today is to

have fun and enjoy playing with my husband."

Then the couple joined a twosome that seemed friendly. Jennifer's anxiety level instantly went up.

Oh no! I need to keep up and play decent golf.

Her heartbeat started racing. Then she thought about the workshop. She checked her grip, focused on the shoulder turn the instructor had told her about, took a couple of deep breaths, and listened to the golf angel whisper in her ear.

"You got this, Jennifer. Remember what the coach told you: It's okay to hit bad shots. Just relax. Your goal is to have fun and keep up with the group in front of us. If you hit a bad shot, you can pick it up. You're a beginner. No need to keep a score until you get better.'"

Jennifer had always felt stressed when playing golf. Today, she was relaxed. When she hit a bad shot, she picked up her ball, enjoyed the walk to the green, dropped off the ball, chipped, and putted. Jennifer played her best! She enjoyed conversation with her playing partners—and the golf angel.

Thoughts Are Just Thoughts

What if Jennifer had listened to the golf devil on her other shoulder? The little devil would have said, "You need to keep up. You play too slow," or "Oh my God! You're horrible. You're not good enough to play on the course." Jennifer would probably have been stressed and too busy dealing with negative talk to play well or enjoy chatting with the guys.

Golf devil and golf angel talk are thoughts in your mind. They tell you different stories about your golf game and you as a person. Which voice would you like to listen to? Of course, you would rather have an angel talk.

We often think our thoughts are us and tend to believe whatever our thoughts tell us. Maybe you're in a bad mood and grumpy, but you don't know why. You listen to the little devil's whisper without even knowing you've done so. Imagine how you would feel and what might happen if you listened to the little devil on your shoulder all day long!

You're not your thoughts!
Thoughts are just thoughts; if you don't like them, you don't have to believe them.

It's Okay to Have Negative Thoughts and Feelings

It may sound counterintuitive, but even the most devout and skilled monks can't avoid negative self-talk. Also, you don't want to resist or push away negative thoughts and feelings if you want to eliminate them. Resistance is just another way of focusing, so when you resist, the thought or feeling tends to stick around.

Just like you push away the thought, *Don't eat the cake in the fridge* when you try to lose weight, the more you resist, the more you think about the cake. You try harder not to think about it, but the image of the cake sitting in the fridge persists. Ultimately, you might lose the battle and eat the cake with guilt. I admit that I've done it more than once.

You might be thinking, *It's easier said than done. How can I stop having negative talk?*

Yes, I agree. It's not easy. But I promise you'll get better at this if you become aware of your thoughts, observe them, and tell yourself, *"Thoughts are just thoughts. You aren't your thoughts."* Then, accept the feelings and let them go as much as you can.

Give yourself permission to have negative self-talk. Remember that the messages you hear are just the little devil's whispers, not who you are. Negative self-talk is just a habit. You can create a new one. It's like building muscles by working out

Tiger's Ten-Step Rule

Every golfer hits bad shots—including Tiger Woods. So when I heard about this simple yet effective drill, I adopted it. I've since shared the tool with many golfers.

When Tiger hits a shot he doesn't like, he lets himself get upset, mad, or whatever he feels while taking ten steps. Then he lets it go and moves on to the next shot. Tiger doesn't push away his negative feelings. Instead, he gives himself time to feel negative emotions and does his best to let them go. Perhaps he knows "what you resist, persists."

Change Your Physiology

Another tool that can be useful is to change your physiology. If you change your physiology, you can change your state of mind. So, when you feel crappy, go for a walk, exercise, or do some physical activity to break the negative state of mind and feel better.

When one of my sons was young, he started having a tantrum. I lifted him and said, "Grab the pull-up bar like a little monkey." He became curious and did as instructed. By the time I put him down on the floor, he had forgotten what he was upset about and was back to being a happy little guy.

What can you do on the golf course to change your physiology? Try jumping jacks, swinging your club backwards, or stretching. You can be creative.

The tools in this chapter can make a big difference in your golf game and life if you keep applying them:

1. **Be aware of your thoughts and observe them without judgment.**
2. **If you catch your negative self-talk, ask yourself if it's true.**
3. **If your answer is yes, ask, "How do you know?"**
4. **Thoughts are just thoughts. You're not your thoughts.**
5. **If you don't like your thoughts, don't believe them.**

And be nice to both the Golf Devil and the Golf Angel because they'll be with you as long as you keep playing golf, no matter how great you become. They're part of you. So treat both of them as your friends.

Chapter 6

Every Shot Counts

"Every shot counts. The three-foot putt is as important as the 300 yard drive."
– Henry Cotton

Golf is a Game of Putting a Ball in a Cup

Obviously, every shot counts in the game of golf, yet we often forget or aren't aware of the concept. Golf is a game that requires you to take as few shots as possible; it's about getting the ball in the cup. You determine your score by writing down the number of shots you take on each hole on the scorecard and totalling them at the end of the game. You don't get points for a beautiful performance like in figure skating. It doesn't even matter how far you hit the ball unless you're in the long drive competition or try to win the long drive in the event. The game sounds simple, but we all know it's complicated.

Many of us love "boring golf." Hit straight, hit the green, and putt. No drama other than what others are experiencing. You're at peace, enjoying the pleasant day. Then suddenly, you get into trouble, and you're sucked into the drama, too. Golf is like life, isn't it? We're delighted when we hit a long solid drive off the tee. We're surprised and excited when we sink a 20-footer for a birdie. But when we hook a shot or miss a three-foot putt, we get upset. Why is that? Why do less than perfect shots take our happiness away from us? To answer such questions, I believe you need to determine why you play golf in the first place. What's your purpose?

Kyle's Story—Chasing Distance

Kyle is an athletic guy who played sports growing up. He played baseball, football, and basketball and was very good at them. He even played football in college. Now Kyle is in his late 20s and decides to take up golf because many of the guys in his circle play.

Golf isn't even a sport. I'm stronger and more athletic than those guys. I know I can quickly get better than anyone.

Kyle begins watching as many golf videos on social media as he can. However, the more he watches, the more confused he becomes. And when

Kyle goes to the range to practice, most of his time is spent hitting the driver. He tries to swing hard to hit over 300 yards, but it never happens. Instead, he sprays all over the place while the guy beside him hits a much longer ball.

This guy is much smaller than me. He even doesn't look like he's swinging hard. Is he hitting over 300 yards? Oh, jeez, crazy! How can he hit that far?

Kyle is fascinated. But that soon turns to frustration.

I should be able to hit longer than this little guy! I need to get better if I'm going to play with my buddies this weekend.

Kyle keeps hitting with a driver until the range balls are gone, and when he finally heads to the golf course, he feels both excited and anxious.

We'll be playing for money, but I should beat all of them, especially Pete. I'm much more athletic. He never played any sports growing up and isn't athletic at all.

But then the guy on the practice range pops up in his mind.

※

On the first tee, Kyle grabs his brand-new driver and swings as hard as possible. Despite the effort, he slices so much that the ball lands in the fairway on the next hole.

Pete's up next and hits a 280-yard drive right down the middle. Kyle's anxiety level starts to rise.

How can he hit 280?

They get on the green, and it's time to putt. Kyle's ball is about 20 feet from the cup.

I should make this.

Except Kyle never practiced putting because he thought it should be easy. His ball passes the cup by six feet.

Oh my God, I putted too hard! Don't 3 putt. You need to make this.

This time he's too careful and putts short, leaving a three-foot putt.

"What are you doing, Kyle? You're an idiot!" he says out loud.

Now he's angry. Kyle stands up over the ball and putts without taking time. His ball misses the cup.

Kyle finishes with a 4 putt and feels miserable.

I should be better than this. I'm athletic. I've been good at every sport I played in my life. Golf isn't even a sport. It should be easy!

He starts wondering if he has enough cash for the bet he will lose with his buddies.

Every Shot Has a Purpose

Your purpose in golf is to hit the ball from point A to B as accurately as possible. However, you don't need to hit solidly from point A to B.

You'll often see the driving range full of people pounding the balls with a driver. Yet you'll rarely see the practice putting green crowded unless there's a competition. It's the opposite at PGA and LPGA tournaments. The pros spend more time on the practice green. That's because "the three-foot putt is as important as the 300-yard drive."

Every shot counts as one stroke, whether it's a 300-yard drive, a 100-yard wedge shot, a chip shot, a bunker shot, or a 3 foot putt. They're all one stroke.

So start with getting to know your game and how you really want to play it. Everyone has a unique purpose for playing golf. You may want to play for fun, enjoying time with your friends and family. Some of you will want to break 90, and some will want to shoot even par. Others of you might want to compete at a high level. A few may even have a dream of playing on the professional tour.

Once you're clear about what your goals and dreams are, what will you do to get there? What's the purpose of every shot? In a later chapter, we'll talk about how to set a clear intention and play the best golf for you.

What Jack Nicklaus Does

Jack Nicklaus said, "I never hit a shot, not even in practice, without having a very sharp, in-focus picture of it in my head. It's like a color movie. First, I 'see' where I want it to finish, nice and white and sitting up high on the bright green grass. Then the scene quickly changes, and I 'see' the ball going there: its path, trajectory, and shape, even its behavior on landing. Then there is this sort of fadeout, and the next scene shows me making the kind of swing that will turn the previous images to reality."

That's one of the reasons Nicklaus became one of the greatest golfers in history. He has never hit a ball without a purpose, not even on the range.

We all can learn from The Golden Bear. His routine for every shot doesn't require you to swing like a tour pro. Everyone at any level should be capable of doing it, although you might need time and patience to practice the routine.

When you're about to hit, ask yourself, *"What is my purpose with this shot? What do I want to accomplish?"* Then, visualize where you want to hit and ask, *"Where is my target?"* Now, see in your mind's eye exactly how you want to perform. Feel it.

If you swing the club, strike the ball, chip, and putt with a clear purpose, you'll play better and score better! And having a clear purpose not only makes you a better golfer, but it also helps you live a better life.

The Miracle Round with Mom

My mom was a tiny lady; I remember she always looked fabulous in stylish golf clothes. Dad played a lot of golf throughout his life for business, but Mom didn't start playing until after their children were old enough to be independent (she was in her late 30s). However, they enjoyed playing together, Dad always taking care of her on the course—even though they often argued like typical golfer couples.

Mom had a slow, beautiful swing that gave her 120 yards when using her driver. She worked at improving, and most people couldn't believe she wanted to break 90. After all, if you can hit only a little over 100 yards with a driver, it's unlikely you'll hit the green in regulation unless on a very short par 3. So how could she expect to play better than bogey golf? The answer is that Mom hit short but very straight, and she became very good at around the green.

Unfortunately, when my mom broke 90 for the first time, I was a teenager who wasn't into golf, and I was clueless about how difficult it is for a lady in her 40s who only hits 120 yards off the tee to break 90. I wish I had known that. I would've celebrated with her.

Mom developed Alzheimer's in her early 70s, and since I live in the US and my parents lived in Japan, I didn't see them often. But late one fall—when her condition worsened, and my dad struggled to take care of her—I decided to visit. Dad called and said, "Believe it or not, Mom wants to play golf. So pack some golf clothes and shoes just in case."

Now, my mother was already so cognitively declined that I wasn't sure if she was capable of playing golf. But I was hoping and thinking, *I want to play golf with Mom one more time,* as I packed my brand-new shoes in my suitcase.

She and Dad came to the airport to pick me up, and a big smile graced her tear-streaked face. This was the mom I knew! But, of course, her condition fluctuated. One moment, she was totally fine; the next, she was someone I had never met. Still, she was determined and persistent that we play golf.

The weather forecast for the next day wasn't very promising, and it rained hard that evening. Mom still didn't change her mind, even when the rain continued into the morning. My dad wasn't sure he wanted to drive more than an hour to the golf course.

"Are you sure you want to play golf?" he asked.

"Yes. I want to go!" Mom exclaimed.

Her voice was filled with excitement, and I wondered if she understood the situation.

Dad shook his head and said, "Okay. Let's go. We can always turn around to come home."

On the way to the golf course, the sun came out. I felt like the Golf God was with us. My mom was alert and excited to play golf. Dad teed up the ball for her on each hole because she wasn't capable, and every time it was her turn to hit, we needed to remind her. Mom's mind seemed foggy, and it was clear that the cruel disease had affected her brain.

But miracles happen! Once Mom addressed the ball, she knew what to do. She became very focused, and we didn't need to tell her what to do. That part of her brain wasn't affected by the disease. Her mind for golf was there, and she enjoyed every shot with purpose! On one of the short par 3s, Mom hit a good straight shot like she used to. Then she hit another excellent shot that landed the ball in the rough just off the green. Her chipping was still in her, and I could see "my mom" before the disease started to destroy her brain. The ball stopped about 5 feet from the cup. Mom took a good stroke with perfect speed and dropped the ball into the cup! I jumped up and down and took many pictures and videos of her. I didn't want to think it was my last round with Mom, but I knew I had witnessed her final bogey. Dad and I enjoyed every moment with her.

My mom played golf with purpose until the last shot on the final hole, and we laughed and had a blast. I believe her goal that day was to play with me because she wasn't even aware of why we were at the airport when I headed back to the US. I'm actually grateful that Mom wasn't sure why I said goodbye to her.

Four months after the miracle round, I jumped on another airplane to be at Mom's funeral. Every shot she made on the last round of her life had purpose and will stay in my heart forever.

Every Shot Starts in Your Mind

Every shot starts in your mind. The entire process until hitting the ball is done there. That means you're the one who makes the decision for every shot—what kind of shot to hit, whether to play safe and lay up or take a risk to position better for the next shot, where to aim, and what club to use. Lastly, you trust your decision and commit to it. All this occurs in your mind, and then you execute with a clear purpose. I promise you'll play better if you follow that routine for every shot! You can be great at this! You don't need to hit a 300-yard drive to be good at golf.

Chapter 7

Think Better, Play Better

"Success depends almost entirely on how effectively you learn to manage the game's two ultimate adversaries: the course and yourself."
– Jack Nicklaus

Emily likes to golf and plays with her friends a couple of times a week. She also enjoys participating in the ladies group fun events. Emily isn't a serious golfer but does want to improve her game. She sometimes takes lessons and practices and believes she'll play better once her swing improves. Accordingly, whenever Emily goes to the range, she only practices "full swing." She doesn't hit long but can hit fairly straight.

One rainy Tuesday morning, Emily looked outside and thought, *Not sure I want to play in Ladies group today. I'm not in the mood. But I just took a lesson and was hitting better on the range yesterday. Maybe I should go.* So, she put on her rain jacket and walked out the door.

The rain had stopped by the time Emily got to the course. It made her feel better. She paired up with her friends and decided it would be a fun day!

Emily started with a decent drive.

Great! My swing is working. The lesson helped me.

The woman walked to her ball with anticipation and grabbed her favorite hybrid. She went through her mental list of how to swing and focused hard on the shot. But unfortunately, Emily was so focused on how to swing that she completely forgot to aim.

"Where are you going?" she cried.

And so the nightmare began. Emily walked to her ball and rushed to chip it. Instead, she chunked the shot, barely got on the green, and left a 40-foot putt.

Oh, my goodness. How can I chip that bad?

She rushed to her ball and putted without taking time. The ball passed the cup ten feet. Now Emily was getting anxious.

I don't want to 3 putt!

She was afraid to putt too hard this time and left it short, a 4-footer.

Panicked, Emily screamed, "I can't 4 putt!"

Emily didn't want to take time to putt because she felt like she would become even more nervous. The ball missed the cup by a hair, and she sheepishly wrote a seven on her scorecard.

I've been working on my game. Why can't I get better?

Does Emily's story sound familiar to you? She doesn't have much holistic knowledge of the golf game. The woman believes she can shoot better scores if her swing improves. She also knows her short game is important but has never thought about working on it. What Emily needs is to improve her "Golf IQ."

What is Golf IQ?

You hit, chip, and putt to put the ball in the cup. You use your body to execute the performance, but thinking is also a big part of this game. So big that you can improve your performance without working on your swing. It's true; thinking about how you play can help you lower your scores.

You might have heard the phrase "Golf IQ." There's no concrete definition, but I believe Golf IQ is the level of knowledge to play the best potential game of golf, including course management/strategy, swing and short game mechanics, preparation for the round, how to practice, the knowledge of how the mind affects your physical game, how to handle emotions, rules, and etiquette. So, how is your Golf IQ? Whatever it is, I promise that your Golf IQ will improve after reading this book. Let's continue to dive!

Conquer the Course with Strategy

Of course, you must keep working on your mechanics to play your best golf. But we're going to focus on the importance of course management here. Because no matter how far you hit, how great your swing, or how killer your putting is, if you manage the course poorly, you won't be able to maximize your ability to shoot a low score. Course management is a key ingredient in scoring well.

Jack Nicklaus said, "Once you play a tournament, you're playing against the golf course, you're playing against yourself and trying to do the best you can." I, too, believe you should always play against the course and yourself if you want to play well. So, let's use our brains to create a strategy to shoot a better score.

Before you create your strategy, you'll want to know your ability and purpose. For example, golfers who play for fun with their golf buddies have a different purpose than competitive golfers. The point is to create a strategy for your ability and purpose to improve your course management skills.

Course Management

Course management is your strategy for playing the course the best you can. It includes a strategy for playing the round, each hole, and every shot with the best decision-making to score as low as possible. Course management will differ for each player, depending on their skills, ability, physical and mental condition, course condition, level of difficulty, and weather conditions.

If you haven't thought about strategy before, this chapter can help you score better. You might even get results in the next round.

What's Your Favorite Yardage?

Note: This section isn't for you if you're an elite player who hits accurately with any club.

Most golfers have a favorite yardage. So why do you like that distance? Chances are it's because you hit better for the distance with your favorite club and trust the shot. However, course management isn't about how you hit; it's thinking about the next shot. You want to think about strategy—where's the best distance, lie, and angle?

Let's use distance as an example. You want to leave your favorite yardage for the next shot whenever possible. In other words, you don't want to leave a distance you aren't comfortable with. That means if you get nervous when facing a 40-yard shot with a half swing and your favorite yardage is 100 yards, you should lay up for the distance.

My golf buddy Rick was a good player with a 6-handicap. One day we were on a short par 5, one of my favorite holes in the world. You can be aggressive and go for the green in 2, but it's risky. You may get in trouble with the shallow green, bunkers, water, and a hazard close behind the green.

After Rick hit a perfect drive down the middle of the fairway, he said, "Give me some tips. I want to make a birdie here."

So, I asked him, "Do you feel comfortable going for the green?"

"No."

"What's your favorite yardage?"

"100 yards. Are you telling me to lay up with a 9 iron?"

He gave me a weird look like he was thinking, *Are you kidding me?*

"Yes," I said. "I'm not kidding."

He shook his head and said, "Okay. I'll lay up then."

Rick hit the perfect shot to leave his favorite distance. Then his 100-yard shot stopped 4 feet from the pin. I grinned, and he sank the putt for a birdie.

Shortly after we played together, Rick broke 70, something he hadn't done for a long time. So if you're puzzled like Rick after I told him to lay up with a 9 iron, remember his story the next time you're playing. Changing up the strategy can help you to score better!

Your Clubs are Part of You

You can't play golf without clubs. They're part of us when we play, so let's get to know them.

- Learn how far you hit with each club and how the golf ball behaves with each. The distance for each club should be "your average distance during the round," not the best solid shot you hit out of 20 shots or the average distance on the range. That's because 80% of your best practice efforts are likely to occur on the golf course 20% of the time.
- Know how you tend to hit with every club.
- How often do you hit well?
- How about the ball flight? Does it draw, fade, hook, slice, or go high or low?
- What's your confidence level with each club?
- What's your favorite club? Like Rick making a birdie from laying up for his favorite yardage, play with your favorite club more often and score better by thinking differently <u>without</u> changing your skills.

Treat every club with love. They're with you every time you play. They're part of you.

Don't Try to Be a Hero. You Aren't Tiger Woods

Alex is a weekend golfer who shoots around 90. He's a bogey golfer who wants to get better and shoot in the 80s all the time and possibly wants to become a single-digit handicapper. But he doesn't think he can improve his game without practicing a lot.

While Alex played with his friends one weekend, he struggled off the tee and got himself in trouble.

"Why can't I play a little better?" he sighed.

He found his ball under the trees. The lie left a tiny bit of room to go for the green, but he would need a precise shot with a low trajectory to hit it.

Alex looked at the ball and thought, *Well, close your eyes and hit it.*

So, instead of thinking about other options, like punching out to the fairway with a safe shot, he took a risk and hit the ball. The ball went high instead of low, hit a tree, rattled between the branches, and settled in an impossible lie. Now he was forced to take an unplayable and had to punch out to get back on the fairway. As you can imagine, he had a typical blow-up hole.

"Why do I always get blow-up holes?" Alex groaned.

His good round was gone.

Dr. Bob Rotella said, "Hit the shot you know you can hit, not the one you think you should." He's absolutely right about this, yet we often try the shot that we might pull off one in 50 times. We see the tour players on TV hit "miracle shots." They seem miraculous to us because we need a miracle or luck to hit those amazing shots. We probably haven't even tried them before, never mind hitting such shots successfully. Conversely, the pros who make these amazing shots know how to do so because they've practiced those exact shots and completed them successfully.

If you're not confident with a tough shot, never try it on the course until you practice and gain confidence in your ability to make it successfully. I know that playing safe doesn't sound very exciting, but it's what you must do if you want to score better. If Alex learned to avoid hitting risky shots and play safe, he would save more than a few strokes, and his handicap would definitely drop. So think twice (or more) before trying to hit the shot that you think requires a miracle.

The Hole with Bad Juju

Are there holes that you always play badly? Do you get bad vibes on those holes or feel the presence of an evil spirit before you even begin to play? If you create such stories, they might just become your reality.

How do you fix the problem? First, you want to figure out WHY you think you suck on the hole. Is the hole more difficult than others? What's your tendency? How's your strategy? What's in your mind before you hit or putt?

Emma hates the 8th hole at her home course.

"Why do I play so bad on this hole every time?" she mutters.

Every time Emma approaches the 8th, she experiences flashbacks of her past performance and begins to feel lousy. Today, Emma tees up the ball, grips the club tightly, and, as expected, hits horribly.

"Not again!" she cries.

With more than 180 yards to the green, Emma grabs her 3 wood and hits it from the rough. She chunks, and it takes her a couple more shots to get on the green.

When Emma has her putter in hand, she screams, "I hate this hole!"

Here are a few things Emma can do to play better and enjoy the hole:

- Focus on what she'll do instead of thinking about what she might do wrong.

- Play conservatively and safely.
- Have a plan regarding how she's going to play. For example, if she usually doesn't hit well with her driver off the tee, she could use her fairway wood for the tee shot.
- Visualize what she wants to do instead of thinking about what she doesn't want to do.
- Relax and make sure to grip the club lightly.
- Let go of the result (good or bad) and move on to the next shot.

I bet many of you have been "Emma." Except there's no evil spirit living on the golf course; it resides in your imaginary world. And as is often the case, whatever you imagine—good or bad—becomes a reality. So why don't we create "La-la land" playing awesome in our minds and turn the hole you hate into the hole you love?

Think Backward From the Green

Does "thinking backward from the green" sound familiar to you? You may not be familiar with the concept, but it's a common strategy among players on the tour. The idea is that you plan to set yourself up for a comfortable shot to the green, which means you set up your second shot to use your best club at your favorite distance from a great lie.

- If you're not an elite golfer, you should aim for the middle of the green or the safest spot.
- If you're not confident with certain shots, like the bunker or flop shot, you need to play to avoid those shots.
- If you're on a par 4, figure out what you want to do off the tee. For example, where do you want to take your second shot from? Not only do you want to land in a safe zone, but you also want to avoid narrow areas, hazards, or bunkers. Be careful to set yourself up for the second shot at your favorite distance, with a better angle to the green and a placement that allows you to avoid trouble. You may not want to use a driver off the tee, depending on the situation.
- If you're on a par 5, aim at the best position so that your second shot reaches the area you need to be in for your third shot. Even if you're on a reachable par 5, you may want to lay up to your comfortable distance. Then, depending on your ability and confidence level, you may make an easy birdie like my friend Rick did.

You want to create a strategy for every hole. Do this, and you'll be surprised at how many strokes you can shave from your score. It's all about better course management.

Where's Your Target?

We're often busy focusing on how to swing before we hit the shot, thinking about what we watched on YouTube last night, analyzing the mistake we just made, carefully going through a checklist of what we need to do to hit the ball, or worrying about hitting a bad shot. And we forget to aim! Have you ever hit an awesome pure shot only to have the ball go somewhere other than where you intended, as if it has a free spirit, and realized you did a sloppy job of aiming at the target?

Pick a small target for every shot as precisely as possible. It's one of the most important aspects of golf and can help you shoot a better score than if you master a beautiful swing or have expensive clubs. The idea is to choose a specific small target above eye level—like a tree or branch or spot on the ground—for every shot.

Your body and brain know how to hit your target more accurately than you think. You can test this by grabbing different sizes, weights, and shapes of objects: a golf ball, car key, crumpled paper, pen, or even a book, and throwing each into a basket from five feet away. Chances are you'll put each object close to or in the basket without thinking about how to throw it. Isn't it amazing that our body and brain can do the job like this? If you pick a specific small target, you may not hit solid, but you'll hit closer to your target than if you have no specific target in mind before you hit the ball.

Check Your Alignment

Poor alignment can cause a poor shot. The following three steps will help you hit better shots and score better:

1. Draw an imaginary line from your target to the ball.
2. Choose an intermediate target on the line about six feet in front of you.
3. Square the club to the target six feet in front of you. Make sure you address the club face before your body.

I've heard one of the top Division One college teams had an "alignment coach." He helped with the team's mental game and alignment. He had coached Tiger Woods when he was a junior player. You may not be able to swing like a tour pro on TV, but I bet you can be as good at setup as any of them.

Create a Pre-Shot Routine Like a Pro's

Have you ever seen the pros on tour rushing to the ball and just hitting it? Probably not. Every one of them has a solid, repeatable pre-shot routine. Why do they do the same thing over and over? Because it helps their game!

I think the importance of pre-shot routines is underrated. A pre-shot routine helps you:

- Focus more.
- Create better tempo.
- Get in the zone.
- Reduce negative or irrelevant thoughts and feelings.
- Perform better under pressure.

Why not take the time to create a solid, repeatable pre-shot routine? You don't have to swing like a pro. You just need a pro's pre-shot routine.

You can mimic the routine of your favorite tour pro and use the following steps:

- The average pre-shot routine time for pros is 25.5 seconds, starting when they pull the club from the bag. When approaching the ball, you may want to think about strategy and plan how to perform to achieve the desired outcome.

- Pick a club for the shot, visualize the shot you want, and pick a target.
- See and feel the shot.
- Take practice swings. Focus on tempo and relax to release the nerves if needed.
- Address the ball, make sure your alignment is square, and see and feel the shot again.
- Take a couple of deep breaths, focus, and execute!

My son, Jack, was getting ready to play his first state amateur tournament as an adult struggling with his swing. He also noticed that his pre-shot routine was getting longer. Jack didn't have enough time to work on his swing, so he shortened his pre-shot routine and focused on it instead. Despite being nervous about playing with grown men in the tournament, Jack finished 67 with 5 under on the last four holes with three birdies and an eagle.

After the round, he said, "I let go of the swing thoughts and just focused on the pre-shot routine, and it worked!"

So, observe and time your pre-shot routine the next time you play. From there, develop a solid, repeatable routine. You might be surprised how much it helps your golf game!

People hardly talk about the post-shot routine, but it's as important as your pre-shot routine. As I mentioned earlier, Tiger's 10-step rule would be helpful after hitting a bad shot or missing a putt. And after every shot or putt—good or bad—give yourself 10 seconds to think and feel about the shot, then let it go and move on to the next shot.

Always Play with a Clear Intention

It's crucial to play every round, hole, and shot with a clear intention. No matter how well you strike the ball or if you're an awesome putter, it would be hard to play your best without clear intentions. Think with a clear intention as much as you can and play better! And remember, if you play better, you'll feel great and be happier, too.

Chapter 8

Do You Hit Crappy Shots?

*"Golf is not a game of good shots.
It's a game of bad shots."*
– Ben Hogan

Everyone Hits Bad Shots

As long as you keep playing, you'll hit bad shots. Even the best players in the world can't avoid hitting them. Bad shots are part of the game of golf.

Here's something interesting. The PGA tour average for:

- 4-foot putts is 91.43%
- 5-foot putts is 80.72%
- 8-foot putts is 52.86%
- Fairway hits is 61%
- Greens hit in regulation play is 64%.

The pros miss almost one out of ten 4-footers, 40% of fairways, and 35% of greens! They're the ones who practice many hours every day and play for a living. Yet they still hit bad shots. So, you may want to compare your commitment and skill to the tour pros. Do you unrealistically expect to hit good shots or make better putts than pros? And instead of chasing good shots, you may want to learn how to handle bad shots instead of avoiding them.

Intentions vs Expectations

When you hit good shots on the range, do you expect to do the same during the round? Do you tend to get upset or frustrated when you don't hit the way you want? If so, why?

For example, James was pumped up to play today because he shot his best 85 last weekend.

He said, "I'm going to play like I did last weekend, maybe better. I know I can do it."

His expectation was through the roof! His warm-up shots on the range were pretty decent, and he putted a few before teeing off.

James' anxiety level went up as he approached the first tee, but he thought, *I hit a perfect drive on the first hole last weekend.*

After a few practice swings, James swung hard to hit long, but his ball arced toward the woods and crossed the line of out of bounds. His heart raced, and his blood pressure began to rise. He grudgingly hit another drive, finished with a triple bogey and headed to the next hole frustrated, angry, and disappointed. He couldn't think straight.

"It's over," James sighed—even though he still had 17 holes to play.

The second hole was a short par 3, one of the easiest holes on the course.

Trying to think a little more positively, he said, "I made an 8-footer and birdied this hole in the last round. I got this."

The shot wasn't as close to the flag as the last time he played this hole, but James was happy to be on the green. His ball was about 20 feet from the cup.

It's pretty straight, he thought. *I can get close enough for a tap-in par.*

Except he putted too hard, and the ball passed the cup by six feet.

He yelled, "What are you doing, James?" Then, "Okay. I got this. I need to make this for a par."

Again, James putted too hard, and the ball passed by a miserable four feet. The man's anger built.

I can't miss this putt. I'm not going to 4 putt!

Careful not to hit too hard, James putted, and the ball stopped a little short of the cup.

"You're such an effing idiot!' he screamed.

Does this story have a familiar ring? Perhaps you've been James or played with someone like

James. You had high expectations from a previous round, even though you can't control outcomes. Most golfers have been in a similar situation when trying to break 90 or 80. We know his pain, don't we?

Of course, we want to hit solid shots, make putts, and shoot better scores. And it's great to set goals and have clear intentions. But there's a little trick you need to learn. You must have intentions and goals, but you also need to learn to let go of expectations for outcomes beyond your control. If you've only hit a great drive once on the range and expect to repeat it on every tee shot during the round, the thought can drive you nuts! If you're standing behind a 5-footer, see the line, and you're determined to make the putt, great! But it's crucial to let go of the expectation for an outcome you cannot control.

Frustration Kills Your Game

If you expect to make that 5-footer without letting go of the outcome, you might get upset and think, *It should've gone in!* or *I could've made it if I didn't hit the ball mark.*

Start using the words "could've" and "should've," and they could take you to a dark place. Because when you use could've and should've, you're talking about the past, and there's nothing you can do about it. You can't go back in time to fix what happened.

Do You Hit Crappy Shots?

So, getting caught up with the previous shots or putts will most likely leave you frustrated or experiencing some other negative emotion. Frustration kills your game. Frustration never helps you to play better. So, what can you do about it? Don't allow yourself to get frustrated? It's easier said than done. You need to recognize that we all get frustrated. And that's okay. Besides, what you resist persists. The thing to do is prevent frustration in the first place. Do your best not to use words like, could've and should've after hitting a bad shot. Observe your thoughts, and remind yourself that you can't change the result. Let it go, then move on to the next shot.

Play Your Best with Bad Shots

As long as we keep playing golf, we'll hit bad shots. So, play your best with bad shots instead of worrying about hitting bad shots or making mistakes. This process can help you play better, especially when you're having an "off day."

- **See the trouble (or obstacle) as a challenge.** When you get in trouble, treat the situation as a challenge instead of getting upset or down on yourself. Then come up with a smart strategy to get out of it the best way you can. Depending on the situation, you may have to plan to go for a bogey or a double bogey, but the key is to minimize the damage after getting in trouble. It can avoid having a blow-up hole.

> *"Anything can happen, so you have to control your attitude and stay strong."*
> *– Jason Day*

- **Don't overthink or overanalyze a bad shot.** You'll have plenty of time to think about that after the round. On the course isn't the time to analyze; you should focus on the next shot.

> *"The most important shot in golf is the next one."*
> *– Ben Hogan*

- **Identify whether or not a bad shot was from an avoidable mistake.** For example, did you hit a bad shot because you were upset and rushed to hit it, made a poor club selection, or didn't take time to aim? You can learn from avoidable mistakes and prevent repeating them.

- **Take deep breaths if you feel negative motions after hitting a bad shot or making a mistake.** Give yourself ten seconds (or ten steps) to feel whatever you are feeling. Then let the emotions go and move on to the next shot.

Do You Hit Crappy Shots?

"Don't let your golf influence your attitude."
– Rory Mcilroy

The Man in the Red Corduroy Pants

Stefan, a young guy from the Bronx, received an invitation to play at a golf event. He had no clue how to play the game but thought it would be fun. It was a small field of only six groups, and they put Stefan in the last group of the event and day so there wouldn't be anyone behind him to hold up. He had no idea what to wear, so when he showed up in red corduroy pants, everyone started making fun of his pants. Stefan's an optimistic guy, so he really didn't care that people were laughing at him.

On the first tee, Stefan realized he didn't know how to grip the club. He asked his caddy, Meghan, who showed him how to grip and patiently helped Stefan with every shot thereafter.

Thank God, I have Meghan as my caddy, he thought.

Of course, everyone except his group finished the day in good time. The sun began to set, and the golfers and their caddies were watching the last group from the back porch terrace of the clubhouse.

That last hole happened to be a par 3. The other golfers in Stefan's group made their tee shots and left him with the final one of the game. When he was setting up at the ball, Meghan told him to aim a little left. Thanks to her, the ball flew straight.

Almost done, he thought.

Everyone watched as Stefan's ball continued to fly true, landed on the green, and rolled toward the hole. And it kept going until his last shot found the hole. The audience started screaming, jumping up and down, and pouring beer on the first-time golfer. Everyone went crazy! The young guy in the red corduroy pants made a hole-in-one on the first round he ever played.

You probably think this was a fictional story that I made up. But it really happened. My friend Meghan caddied for Stefan. It's one of the most amazing golf stories I've heard.

We all hit bad shots, but you never know what will happen with the next one. If you learn to mentally and emotionally handle those bad shots, you'll play better and enjoy the game more—even when you're not striking the ball well or your short game is off. The mind is powerful, and your golf experience can vary greatly depending on your chosen state.

"Your next shot is a new experience.
It might be the best shot you ever hit in your life."
– Harvey Penick

Chapter 9

Unlock the Possibilities

"When you look at the possibilities instead of the problems, the future is filled with endless opportunities."
– Zig Ziglar

What's your wild dream as a golfer? Do you wish you could be a scratch golfer, even though you've been shooting around 90 for decades? Do you fantasize about hitting 280 yards but have never hit longer than 200 yards? Do you believe you can make it happen, or does your inner voice tell you it's impossible?

Audrey Hepburn said, "Nothing is impossible. The word itself says, 'I'm possible.'"

I like that. It's a great way to change your perspective and focus, which is crucial because from the first moment you think or say "impossible," you begin to create that reality.

Would you believe there's a 92-year-old lady who gets up at 4:20 in the morning, runs for a couple of hours and works out for four to five hours daily?

92-year-old Japanese female fitness instructor, Taki Mika

Her name is Mika Takishima. A petite 92-year-old Japanese lady who stands 4'10" and weighs 92 lb, she's radiant, has a positive vibe, and her beautiful energy is contagious.

Mika was a typical Japanese housewife for her generation and raised her children and cared for her husband. When she was 65, comments by her family made Mika realize she had gained 40 lbs, so she started taking weight training, swimming, and aerobics classes at a nearby gym. Mika enjoyed the workout and quickly saw results.

One day, her personal trainer asked her to teach the class without warning. Mika told him there was no way she could teach, but he put the microphone on her anyway.

She hesitated and said, "Okay, I can do 10 minutes."

Her instructor replied, "You'll teach for 45 minutes."

Mika taught the class perfectly, and an 87-year-old instructor was born! She plans to continue teaching for as long as possible, maybe even until she turns 100.

Mika goes to bed at 11 pm, gets up at 3:30 am, and runs and walks for two hours—every day. She works out for five hours—every day. Mika has no pain, takes no medication, and doesn't use supplements because she eats healthy balanced food.

"Age is just a number," she says. "No matter how old you are, start working out, and you'll get better."

Mika's a true inspiration. She proves that anything is possible!

Everything Starts From Within

Do you think you can make your wild dream come true? If your answer is yes, great! If your answer is still no, what makes you feel you can't achieve it? What stops you from becoming the golfer you want to be?

Some of you might think things like:

- *I'm not talented enough to become a single-digit handicapper.*
- *I'm getting old. I'll get weaker and worse every year.*

- *I didn't start young enough to be a great golfer. You need to start young if you want to be good at the game.*
- *I'm not athletic, and I've got no hand-eye coordination.*

Those negative thoughts (limiting beliefs) are in your way! Please go back to Chapter One and complete the beliefs exercise. Reframing limiting beliefs is one of the biggest keys to closing in on success in golf and life, so don't skip this process!

Note: Once you've chosen your new beliefs, you can reset your goals and dreams if necessary.

- **The dream**

To construct specific plans to make your dream come true, you'll need clarity. Grab a pen and paper and write down what you know about your golf game. Write whatever comes to your mind. Don't judge what you put down.

Then, ask some questions:
- What do I want to improve?
- What do I want to achieve?
- What's my dream?

- **Make the impossible possible**

Once you're clear about your dream, dive into making it happen with the positive mindset you developed when reframing your beliefs. What do you need to work on to make the improvements you identified? Be specific (e.g. I want to break 80 over the next two months by improving my long putts and straightening my drive). Once you set clear goals like this, it's time to plan how to get there.

Important note: If you start doubting, feel uncertain, or have negative thoughts like, *I don't think I can get better,* or *No way, it's not going to work,* then please do the reframing exercise in Chapter One again and create smaller goals.

- **Make effective plans**

You must be specific on how to work on your game. That doesn't mean you need to practice for hours every day like a pro on tour. Make plans that work for you:
  - What do you want to improve?
  - What actions do you need to take to improve?
  - Do you need to work on your short game?
  - On your swing?
  - What about course management?
  - If you start having negative thoughts like, *I'll never get better,* do the reframing exercise again and create a smaller goal.

- **Always practice with purpose**

Every time you practice, do so with specific plans and purpose. Practice mindfully. For example, if you're working on your swing after taking a lesson, focus on what you want to achieve with clear intention and an eye on the outcome you want. We often "forget" the intention and practice mindlessly.

- **Quality over quantity**

  I sometimes see golfers pounding the balls mindlessly on the driving range. If you're not aware of your goal (the reason you're practicing) and just hit the balls repeatedly, you can't improve your game and risk creating a bad habit and getting worse. Also, practicing with purpose for a short period is better than mindless long practice. Even if you only have 15 minutes to practice, you should still focus on your goal.

- **Be gentle with yourself**

  Don't criticize yourself when you're not doing as well as you want or expect or if you find that you've stopped working on your game. It happens, and it's okay. It's even okay to feel down about it. We all do that sometimes. The best course of action is to accept what happened, let it go, and move on.

- **Take baby steps**

  Take small steps towards your goal. We all go up and down, and sometimes we doubt our abilities and our future. It's okay. The important thing is to keep on going. Never give up. If you stop working on your game or go back to your old habits, don't beat yourself up with guilty thoughts like, *I can't commit. I'm such a loser!* Instead, reset and start over.

"Baby steps count as long as you are going forward. You add them all up, and one day you look back, and you'll be surprised at where you might get to."
– Chris Gardner

Practice in Your Mind

Some experiments involve practicing only in the mind to improve skills. Piano, free throw for basketball, and muscle mass studies come to mind...

- In a piano skills study, the participants were divided into two groups. One group physically practiced piano while the other only practiced in their mind (mental rehearsal). Both groups practiced two hours per day for five days. Interestingly, the study showed that both groups improved to the same degree, and brain scans showed that both groups developed the same number of new brain circuits.
- In a study by Dr. Biasiotto at the University of Chicago, participants were split into three groups and tested on how many free throws they could make. Then, he had the groups do the following:

Group 1: Practiced free throws for an hour every day.
Group 2: Visualized themselves making free throws.
Group 3: Did nothing to improve their skills.

He retested the participants after 30 days and discovered the following:

Group 1: Improved by 24%.
Group 2: **Improved by 23% (without touching a basketball)!**
Group 3: Didn't improve.

There's even an experiment where people who worked out in their minds gained muscle mass—without lifting weights. So don't underestimate mind power.

If you want to improve your golf game (or any area of your life), mentally rehearse the "best you" for the circumstance and grow new brain circuits. Major James Nesmeth, who played golf repeatedly in his mind for seven years, proved to us that mental rehearsal works!

But what if you're a golfer who doesn't practice and just plays for fun? Great! I hear this from many golfers. I think everyone has a different purpose for playing golf, and no one should judge. However, if you play for fun without working on your game, you may want to have no expectations to play good or bad. Doing otherwise will make it challenging to play for fun and be a happy golfer.

In the next chapter, let's dive into the short game. It's one of the keys to shaving strokes off your game. And we're happier when we shoot a better score, aren't we?

Chapter 10

The Secret of Golf

"The secret of golf is to turn three shots into two."
– Bobby Jones

Do you want to shoot a lower score? I would be shocked if you said no because whether you play for fun or competitively, we all want to play at our best. But despite that often strong desire to do better, most don't have a specific effective strategy for improving their game to lower scores. So I have a suggestion, and it's golf's secret: **The main key to shooting a better score is to improve your short game!** Why is it so important? Because more than half of the shots during a round are made within 100 yards. As Bobby Jones once said, "The secret of golf is to turn three shots into two." The way to do that is to improve your short game.

65% of Shots are Within 100 Yards

Research shows that about 65% of shots take place within 100 yards. Think about that statement. How many times during a round do you use a driver? Statistics say 13. That means that if your average score is 90, your drives account for approximately 15% of your shots. And most golfers use a putter to hit the ball more than twice as much as a driver. Conclusion? If you want to improve your game, practice your short game.

What do many golfers complain about? Their drive! But if you improve your short game, you'll score better—even when your long game is off. Intuitively, most of us know that working on the short game is crucial to improving our scores. Yet the driving range is often full while practice greens stand empty. So, instead of waiting, why not take advantage of the practice green when no one is there?

40% of Golf is Putting

Almost half of the round is putting. As mentioned in an earlier chapter, the 3-foot putt is as vital as the 300-yard drive. Both shots are one stroke, but we often get more upset when we miss a 4-footer than hitting a drive into the trees. That's because the tendency is to think that making a short putt is easier than hitting a good drive. However, even PGA tour players miss one out of four 5-foot putts. You may not think you're a good putter when you consistently miss 5-footers by a hair, but I'll bet you're better than you think. So, as counterintuitive as it may seem, the way to become a happy golfer is to lower your expectations, avoid frustration, and improve your game within 100 yards.

Know Your Game Within 100 Yards

Write down everything you know about your golf game within 100 yards (and, of course, you can apply this exercise to other areas of your game)—wedge shots, pitch shots, chipping, flop shots, bunker shots, putting, course management, club selection, and the mental part of the game. What are your strengths and weaknesses? Sort them out and make a list. What do you need to improve on the most to score better? How are you going to work on that?

Take your time and dig deeper. Because if you want to improve your game, you must understand precisely what you need to improve upon and draft effective plans to achieve those goals, depending on your purpose for playing golf and your lifestyle. Even if you're a recreational golfer who plays with your buddies over the weekend, the odds are that you want to improve your score and make your buddies buy you a beer, right?

How to Turn Three Shots into Two

There are many ways to turn three shots into two. For example, better course management, avoiding extra strokes with penalty shots, improving your swing to hit more solid and consistent shots, and hitting more greens in regulation. But focusing on the shots within 100 yards can be the best and fastest way.

Practicing with the intent to improve your short game will sharpen your focus, increase your confidence, and improve your score, even on an "off day." Does that make sense to you? If so, why not take steps to improve your short game?

Create little games to challenge yourself:

- Set a goal for total putting strokes.
- How do you want to get up or down when you miss the green?
- How many greens will you hit within 100 yards?
- How close will you get from a certain distance?

You can be creative and create your own game, the one that's best for you. And if you "win" that game, give yourself a little reward. You can also play a friendly side game with your friends and encourage each other.

Practice Putting!

If you don't regularly practice putting or are unsure about your putting stroke, you may want to take a putting lesson. You may not believe it now, but one good short-game lesson can lower your score!

You can also practice putting at home. If you don't have a putting mat, carpet will do. I recommend practicing your stroke using a mirror and ruler as practice devices. Filming your stroke also gives you instant feedback.

It's not necessary to practice for hours (unless you want to). Just set a timer and practice for 5 to 10 minutes. The key is to practice often.

Access Your Inner World

Mechanics and techniques are, of course, important, as you must develop some fundamental skills. But don't forget your inner world—the creative mind and imagination. They're a big part of golf, especially with the short game.

When playing, do your best to let go of the mechanical thoughts and focus on mental rehearsal.

How do you want to perform? Where do you want to land? Do you need the ball to roll or stop short? Ball flight and spin? How close do you want to hit? How about putting? Use imagination to *see* how the ball rolls toward the cup.

Never second-guess yourself; trust your instinct. Studies have demonstrated that your first read or thought is often the right one. Your mind is powerful!

Your Brain and Body Know More Than You Think

I mentioned this earlier. Now, I want you to try an experiment.

Put a basket five feet in front of you. Have some different objects beside you—a golf ball, rock, crumpled paper, key, book, pen, scissors, etc. Throw those objects into the basket. I bet you would have no problem throwing them without thinking much. You wouldn't figure out how to throw them with perfect form, but your brain and body know how much power you need to throw the golf balls compared to the crumpled paper. In a situation like this, a lack of self-confidence might cause mistakes more than your lack of skills. Trust your brain and body! They're more awesome than you believe. So next time you putt or chip during the round, let your brain and body do the job—just like throwing an object into the basket.

Everything starts with your mind—decision-making like club selection, course management, how to swing and putt, and even how you feel. In the next chapter, we'll go deeper into our Zen-like mind.

Chapter 11

Get into the Zone with a Zen-Like Mind

"Golf is a spiritual game. It's like Zen. You have to let your mind take over."
– Amy Alcott

What is Zen?

I grew up in a Buddhist family. We had a beautiful home shrine and chanted a Buddhist sutra for about 20 minutes before dinner each day. As a child, sometimes I didn't appreciate this custom, especially when hungry. I didn't think there was much meaning to the ritual. But looking back, I think I still found serenity, mindfulness, and spirituality at an unconscious level—even though I often thought about dinner while chanting.

Close to 70% of Japanese are Buddhists, so it has become ingrained in our culture. There are also many forms of Buddhism; ours wasn't a Zen sect. However, in Japan, we use words from Zen, like "Mu no Kyochi" or "Mushin," in daily life. It means a state where your mind isn't fixed on or occupied by any thought or emotion. This state of mind requires the absence of the ego or limited self and creates pure mental clarity. Your mind is fully present, aware, and free. I think the Zen-like mind concept was seeded in me early in life, but I didn't "get it" until much later.

What is "Being in the Zone?"

Golfers use the term "get in the zone." You may also have heard it called the "flow state." Most of us have experienced this magical state at one time or another, and it feels terrific! So, I'm not surprised that golfers sometimes chase it.

According to Wiktionary, the zone is a mental state of focused concentration on the performance of an activity in which one dissociates oneself from distracting or irrelevant aspects of one's environment. You'll experience a complete sense of tranquility when you're in the zone, yet you remain aware of what's going on. Many report the world going silent and everything shifting to slow motion as if time itself has slowed. Everything seems easy. You'll feel great, experience a sense of joy, and can perform at your best.

Get into the Zone with a Zen-Like Mind

A 104-degree Fever Put Me in the Zone

A long time ago, when I was a new competitive golfer, I played in a two-day competition in our town. I recall playing okay and leading after the first day. On the second fine summer day, I was playing well, but as we made a turn, something went wrong with my body. A horrible chill set in, and I began shaking. My entire body was in pain.

I told my competitors, " I'm getting very sick. I should go home."

One of them said, "Kumiko, you're leading the tournament. There are just nine more holes. You should keep going."

The pain was awful. When it wasn't my turn, I sat on the ground, thinking, *This is stupid. I should go home.* Or at least I did that until I got so sick I couldn't think.

I'm unsure how, but I kept going and finished the round. When we got to the table to turn in our scores, I was in such a state that I had completely lost track of what I had shot. Imagine my surprise when my opponent said, "You shot even par on the back. I think you won!"

What a painful win. I had a 104-degree temperature, and my body hurt so much that I stopped thinking and played unconsciously. However, because my mind was empty and I was forced to play that way, I ended up in the zone.

I don't recommend playing golf when you're sick; they rushed me to the ER with a kidney infection. And while it wasn't worth the risk to my health to keep playing, that was the only time I played with a completely empty mind and the longest I ever stayed in the zone.

Please don't be silly like me! Let's talk about how to get in the zone in a healthy way.

Give Yourself Permission to Make Mistakes

Fear is guaranteed to mess up your golf game and never helps you to get in the zone. It may sound strange to suggest that you give yourself permission to make mistakes. I can also tell you it's not easy to do. But let me ask: Have you played better and felt free when you just played golf, didn't keep a score, and focused on enjoying the course? And have you been so nervous about the possibility of missing a 4-footer that would give you the best score of your life that your body tensed up and you missed the putt?

Okay. Imagine a 4-inch-wide line painted on the floor. Walk along it—one foot at a time, then jump up and down without losing your balance. I'm not asking you to flip as a gymnast does. Just jump on that line. It shouldn't be that hard, should it?

Now, imagine doing the same thing on a 4-inch wide gymnastic balance beam 10 feet off the floor. Can you walk along it and jump up and down without losing balance? Probably not. I couldn't do it. I would be nervous and sweaty, walking ever so slowly, and might not even be able to jump.

Yet it takes the same skill to walk on a 4-inch-wide line, whether on the floor or 10 feet in the air. So why the different results? It's because we give ourselves permission to make mistakes on the floor, but we can't bring ourselves to do the same on the beam 10 feet off the ground. We do fine on the floor but panic on the beam. The fear messes us up.

This is an excellent metaphor for your golf game, and it's why you should allow yourself to make mistakes.

Magic Pills Can't Get You in the Zone, but Your Mind Can

When you're in the zone, it's like being on autopilot. Everything goes well. It feels easy. Simple. Effortless. You stay calm without forcing anything. So gentle and still. Not many thoughts. No complication. You feel incredible, don't you? And golf is much more fun when you're in that state of mind.

But then you wonder, *Golf is so easy. Why can't I*

play like this every time I play?* Or you think, *I got this. I might shoot the best score ever today.* Or maybe, *What's going on here? This can't be happening. It'll end soon.* And the magical spell disappears.

We've all had this experience and would give anything to return to the zone. Unfortunately, the more we try to get back there, the worse our chances are. Oh, how we wish there were a magic pill that we could pop in our mouths to get back to that magical moment! But there isn't. Getting into the zone is a skill you have to learn.

You might be thinking, *That's easier said than done.*

I hear you and would ask that you don't be too hard on yourself. Getting into the zone is all about awareness. Here are some things to practice:

- The first step is to observe your thoughts, emotions, and behavior while playing golf. For example, if you have thoughts about previous shots (good or bad) or worry about shots you haven't hit yet, your thinking is focused on the past or future, not the present moment.
- Once you've identified your thought patterns, the next step is to shift your focus to the here and now—because focusing on staying in the moment is the key to getting into the zone.

- We're all human. Imperfect. So just do your best! If you rush, there'll be no chance of getting into the zone. SLOW DOWN everything (unless you're playing speed golf!)—walking, talking, selecting clubs, even the tempo of your swing, especially if you feel like you're rushing.
- Be aware of your breathing. One of the quickest and easiest ways to slow down and clear your mind is to take several deep breaths, exhaling slowly each time. It can reduce your heart rate quickly, which helps to calm you.
- Relax your body and mind. It's unlikely you'll get into the zone if you overthink, your mind is going crazy with anxiety and stress, and your body is tense. Meditation and anchoring are techniques you can learn that can help you to relax before or while playing golf.
- Play with a clear intention without expectation for outcomes you can't control. Playing with intention is about being engaged and committing to a plan or purpose (e.g., I'm going to lay up so I can use my seven iron to get on the green). It's about concentrating on what you're doing.

Having expectations means you're out of the present moment. Your mind is on the future instead of what you need to do right now. Expectation, especially for outcomes you can't control, leads to frustration. And frustration never helps you to get into the zone or play well.

- Acquire soft focus using peripheral vision. You use peripheral vision to drive a car. You can't drive without it because you need to focus on where you're going and also know what's happening around you—the movement of other cars, objects that shouldn't be on the road, approaching signs you must obey, weather changes, etc. Your subconscious mind takes you over many such mundane tasks while you focus on the more critical challenges of operating a car, like staying on your side of the road or navigating. You don't think about how to push the gas pedal or turn unless you're a brand-new driver because most of us depend on our "autopilot" when we drive. Peripheral vision puts you in a light trance that makes it easier to do all these tasks at once. So, when you pick a target and aim at it, focus on the target but also be "aware" of your surroundings.
- And last but not even close to least, feel the wind and enjoy the sunshine, or if it's raining, smell the fresh air and listen to the birds chirping. Embrace the moment. Enjoy being in nature while on the course, and appreciate how lucky you are to be there.

A Word of Advice

Don't purposely try to get in the zone. It's tempting, but having that thought means you're thinking about the future and have already kicked yourself out of the present moment. Instead, trust the best version of YOU. It's already there. You may not be able to play like a tour pro, but you can bring your best game to the round. Believe in yourself. You're more than you think you are!

Use Your Favorite Music and Get Into the State of Mind You Want

Do you have songs that bring back specific memories or emotions? Sometimes they're great memories, and sometimes they're not. For example, I have songs that bring me back to childhood, while others evoke memories of my wild college party days. But one song that brings up the past vividly is *Careless Whisper* by George Michael. Whenever I hear or think about it, I'm catapulted back to the day my house burnt down. I'm not sure, but I think I was listening to *Careless Whisper* on the way home from college after getting the news from my dad. It's been over 30 years, but the song still evokes vivid memories of that five-hour drive on snowy winter roads.

People often return to the intense emotions and behaviors they experienced during memorable events when some aspect of what happened occurs in the present. These present-day stimuli are called triggers. In PTSD, a loud noise might trigger an extreme response in a soldier who was caught in an explosion during deployment many years ago, just as gazing into the eyes of a newborn might cause intense emotions to well up in a grandmother.

Triggers happen at a subconscious level and are formed haphazardly by life. However, it has proven possible to create them intentionally for a purpose. This is accomplished through a process where a trigger (like a song) is "anchored" to a specific state of mind:

- **Step 1.** Pick a song.
- **Step 2.** Choose the state of mind you want to anchor. Do you want to be calm and relaxed? Or do you want to be focused? What about emotions? Do you want to be confident, strong, and unstoppable?
- **Step 3.** Listen to the song you want to anchor while you imagine playing an amazing round of golf. You're calm. Relaxed. Confident. You feel strong, and your swing is easy. You're having fun. You're unstoppable. On top of the world!
- **Step 4.** Take a break and repeat Step 2 until you can consistently enter the same state of mind

when you listen to that song.
- **Step 5.** Listen to the song or play it in your mind when you want to get into that flow state or zone on the golf course. It will trigger the thoughts and emotions you anchored to the song.

This is a fun tool to improve your mental game. So lighten up and be playful!

Note: Just about anything can serve as a trigger, and you can set up multiple triggers for a particular frame of mind. Also, you can "anchor" with your fingers. I know someone who went into a deep meditative state and pressed his right forefinger to his right thumb. He did this many times over a period of weeks. After that, when he found himself in a stressful situation, he pressed the same finger and thumb together and instantly returned to the anchored state. Over the years, when regular use of the trigger diminished its power, he simply repeated the original anchoring process.

⊶⇝⦆·⦅⇜⊷

I believe playing golf and living life with a Zen-like mind is one path to increased happiness. It's simple, yet not easy. But if you practice the techniques I've described daily, you'll become a happier golfer and a more beautiful soul.

Chapter 12

Golf Is Like Life

"Golf is the closest game to the game we call life. You get bad breaks from good shots; you get good breaks from bad shots—but you have to play the ball as it lies."
– Bobby Jones

Golf is a Special Game

There's no other sport you can enjoy playing with a little toddler, a 90-year-old guy, and a tour pro in the same group. You also can play by yourself. And you get to enjoy conversation with the playing partners even during the competition.

Once, I went to play with a friend at the course in town. It's a busy course. When we were standing on the first tee, a guy in a golf cart came by and asked with a friendly smile, "Can I join you guys? I am going to play only 9 holes."

Of course, we were more than happy to play with him.

He said, "I'm in my 90s and can't see very well. Could you watch my ball?"

He looked to be in pretty good shape for his age. I was amazed and remember thinking, *I hope I will be like him when I'm in my 90s!*

It was a pleasure to golf with this friendly guy, but he didn't need much help from us. He hit straight and long with a beautiful swing. When we were on a par 3, he hit a good shot but was a little short off the green. He chipped perfectly, and his ball stopped a few feet from the cup. Then he made a putt for a par! My friend and I were more excited about his par than he was.

But my best memory of golf is the time I was on the course with my sons when they were young, and it has nothing to do with the game. We went out on a beautiful summer evenings looking for deer, trying to catch a salamander, and picking blackberries. It was such fun watching the boys play in the bunkers. These memories beat winning the tournament I told you about or shooting the best score of my life. I experienced so much love and joy with my babies.

Golf is more than the game. Golf is life.

Money Can't Buy Happiness or Your Golf Game

No matter how much money you have in your bank accounts, happiness and your golf game aren't for sale. I once played with a billionaire (I happened to be there and was asked to join him and his friends) while actively competing in the amateur field.

At one point, he said, "I wish I could play like you."

But you can't buy your golf game.

Happiness is an inside job. Feelings create happiness, and they come from within you. One of the things you can do to make yourself feel better and happier is to express gratitude. If you're not feeling great on the course or in daily life, find three things you're grateful for.

Don't make the mistake of chasing happiness. Every moment is fresh and new, so do your best to be in that moment and choose happy thoughts. You have choices. You can create anything within yourself.

Golf Teaches

Golf teaches us valuable life lessons. Patience. Humility. Honesty. Respect. Kindness. Acceptance. It also teaches you how to let go, be present, problem-solve, and love yourself.

- **Patience**

  Patience is one of the keys to playing great golf. If you lose patience, you could get frustrated, which never helps your golf game. Patience is vital to your success and happiness in life, as well. Impatience is a habit, and so is patience. Isn't it terrific that you can practice patience through golf?

- **Humility**

  If you play golf, the game has humbled you. That's because no one can always play well without bad rounds. Each of us must face the reality that we will make mistakes, play horribly, and suffer losses. However, we learn from these experiences and go back and do what we can to play better. The game is so fluid that, in the long run, the committed golfer learns humility, to improve regardless of what we face, and hopefully become a better person.

- **Honesty**

  Golf is a game of honesty and integrity. It encourages you to be honest with yourself first, your golf game second, and then with others. Jack Nicklaus said, "If there is one thing golf demands above all else, it is honesty." What a great lesson!

Honesty is the secret to happiness on and off the golf course.

- **Respect and Kindness**

Golf teaches us to respect the game and the course, be kind to others and ourselves, not judge, and treat everyone equally. That's also a recipe for an honorable life.

- **Acceptance/Let Go**

Accept what already happened (the past) and let it go. Accept uncertainty, the things that haven't happened yet (the future).

Let go of the expectations for the outcomes you can't control. And as you keep practicing acceptance and learn to let go, you'll become mentally and emotionally stronger; you'll be resilient in golf and life. The process will help you become calmer and kinder to others. You'll also experience less stress and be happier.

- **Be Present**

Accept what it is, let it go, and be present as much as possible. As mentioned in the previous chapter, when your mind is fully present, aware, and free of clutter (noise), you can get into the zone on the course and in life.

- **Problem-Solve**

You'll make mistakes as long you keep playing golf. No golfer can avoid them. So, instead of assuming you'll experience bad results from those mistakes or the trouble you get into, why not see those situations as challenges and figure out what you can do to make the best of them? Tiger Woods has said, "I smile at obstacles." Learn how to be responsive rather than reactive.

Golf never stops teaching us many valuable life lessons, whether you're a tour pro or have just started playing golf. You'll keep discovering new things about yourself (and often about your playing partners). A terrific way to learn to love yourself!

Golf is My Therapist

I think of golf as my therapist, and it has taught me many things:

- Golf has supported me and saved me from drowning in life.
- Sometimes, golf gives me tough love.
- Whenever I'm having challenges, I choose a time when there aren't many people on the course, and I play alone. Sometimes, I have conversations with myself. Other times, I try to empty my mind and

use all my senses to enjoy nature. There are even times when I talk with something out there that's bigger than me—God, the Universe, a great Spirit, your Higher Self. I believe they're all One.
- I see golf as a spiritual game. When we get in the zone, it feels like something beyond a physical game; I feel like someone or something bigger than myself is in and playing through me.
- This game can be harsh and unfair. You may feel defeated, beat yourself up, and want to quit like you do in life. But in golf, I suggest you keep coming back because no sooner than you put aside the thought of quitting, you'll be rewarded with a great round (and forget the bad one). It's a pattern you'll repeat as long as you keep playing golf, and you'll keep creating stories about the game of golf.
- Golf has made me a stronger, better human being.

The game is my therapist.

Love Yourself. Love the Game

If you're reading this last chapter, you must love golf. At least, I hope you do. And I believe everyone has different reasons to love and play the game. But it doesn't matter why you play. If you love the game, keep playing!

People tend to be too hard on themselves on and off the golf course. We sometimes bully ourselves and say mean things during the round. But no matter how you get sick of yourself, you're with yourself 24/7 until your last day on Earth. So be kind, and treat yourself as your best friend.

I believe that words have energy and suggest that you be mindful of the word choices you think and use during the round (and your day-to-day existence). If you use positive words, your mental game is sure to improve. And if you love and are gentle with yourself, you'll play better golf, enjoy the game more, and become happier in life.

Everything starts with your mind. Love yourself. Love the game.

About the Author

You never know how your life will unfold. It likely won't go, or hasn't gone, how you thought it would. That's the way life was for me. I never imagined living in the U.S. or coaching golfers. I couldn't speak English and didn't like golf until my twenties, although my dad was in the golf business.

I came to the U.S. with four little boxes and a suitcase, intending to explore this country for a year and return to Japan to live the rest of my life. The plan was to teach "Koto," a Japanese musical instrument I had played since childhood, but I didn't speak much English and was terrified to answer the phone. Just the thought of asking to buy meat by the pound from the butcher at the grocery store was too much for me.

Yet I'm still here in the U.S. some thirty years later. I never moved back. I have two amazing sons; they're also golfers who improved their golf game so quickly people couldn't believe it. That's the incredible power of the mind!

I never became a professional golfer, but I loved to compete in the amateur field. One of my memorable tournaments was a televised team match called Albertson's Team Championship when I was eight months pregnant with my first child. The competition brought professional golfers and men's and women's club champions together to compete. I played exceedingly well, but our team lost in the semifinal—which is just as well since my baby was born right after the match. The prize I received from the tournament was a gift card for Albertson's grocery store, and I used it to buy diapers and baby food. But my greatest memory from those years is that my sons learned how to play golf in my tummy and went on to become plus handicap golfers.

Having been interested in the mind and body since my early years, I was open-minded to psychology, religion, spirituality, metaphysics, or anything else that could help me improve myself. Whenever I go through challenges in my life, I read self-help books and listen to whatever might help me to get through the tough times. I'm a self-help book junky!

I remember struggling as a tennis player when I was in high school, primarily due to the mental side of the game and a lot of injuries. When I began playing serious golf, it didn't take me long to conclude that the mind played a vital role in this sport, too. I didn't think it would be hard to become

About the Author

a single-digit handicapper in one year if I practiced and played often, so I did it. That was my aha moment. It proved to me just how powerful the mind and beliefs are.

My passion is to help people, and at that time in my life, I was still looking for something I could do to make it happen. That pursuit led me to NLP, which I used to break 70. I immediately went back to my trainers and got certified. My first customer was a beautiful friend in her twenties who struggled with her weight. After just a few sessions, she began losing weight without dieting. And she lost more than 40 lbs in one year.

Since then, I've coached high school athletes in baseball, basketball, running, and skiing. But I eventually decided to focus on golfers. You see, I was already a low-handicap, recreational golfer who could relate to golfers at any level playing with any purpose.

I coach holistically. And although everything starts with the mind, I help my clients get to know their golf game, identify their strengths and weaknesses, dig into their limiting beliefs and reframe them, handle emotions, set goals, work on their skills (swing, short game) using their mind, learn course management (practical, mental, and emotional parts), and play with intention and purpose for every shot and round. Many clients call me the "golf therapist," and I believe this is my calling.

I think of golf in the same way I think of life because it's much deeper than a sport. I remember vividly the time I was playing with friends on a par 3 at my home course, and I told them without much forethought, "I want to write a book about golf and life." But it wasn't until my dad passed away more than 25 years later that I started writing this book. He made it possible, so I dedicate this book to him.

I lived 5,008 miles away from my parents. They were always in my heart, though, and they'll continue to live there forever. My dad left my sons and me a special place called the "Pumpkin Ridge Golf Club." It has hosted many memorable tournaments, including Tiger Woods' last amateur tournament, but the club is magical to me because of countless personal memories with family and friends.

Printed in Great Britain
by Amazon